THE **UKE** OF **WALLINGTON**

Mark Wallington is the author of the bestselling travel books *500 Mile Walkies* and *Boogie up the River*, both of which became radio series. His first credit as a scriptwriter was for *Not the Nine O'Clock News*. He has also written two novels, which he later adapted for television: *The Missing Postman* and *Happy Birthday Shakespeare*. In 1997 *The Missing Postman* won the British Comedy Award for Best Comedy Drama.

In 2005 he published *The Day Job*, an account of his years as a jobbing gardener in north London. He has also written a number of film scripts for television, including *Station Jim* in 2000, and *The Man Who Lost His Head*, in 2007.

THE UKE OF

WALLINGTON

ONE MAN AND HIS UKULELE ROUND BRITAIN

MARK WALLINGTON

Published by AA Publishing, a trading name of AA Media Limited,
Fanum House, Basing View, Basingstoke, Hampshire, RG21 4EA, UK.
Registered number 06112600.
www.theAA.com

First published in 2012
10 9 8 7 6 5 4 3 2 1

A CIP catalogue record for this book is available from the
British Library.

ISBN: 978-0-7495-7273-0

Cover design by Two Associates
Typeset by Bookwork Creative Associates
Printed and bound in the UK by Clays Ltd

A04796

To F & D

Thanks for the Music

CONTENTS

chapter one

hello brighton

Open Mic Tonight, said the sign on the door of the Three Graces, *No poets*. Well, you've got to draw the line somewhere, haven't you?

I was standing outside, trying to convince myself this was a good idea. It was the first night of my nationwide tour and I'd chosen the Three Graces because it was on the edge of town; it would be a forgiving sort of place; I could ease myself in gently. So why did it feel like the entrance to Dodge City saloon? One accidental poem and I'd be a dead man.

I walked in and all eyes were on me. This could have been because I was a stranger in town or because I had a ukulele slung over my shoulder.

The barmaid said, 'Open mic?'

There was still time to pull out.

'Johno!' she yelled.

A man with nose jewellery shook my hand and eyed the ukulele. His look was quite probably welcoming, but all it said to me was: you do know that a) you're 30 years older than our average performer, and b) the last ukulele player we had in here got such a hard time from this crowd he left his clothes on the beach and was never seen again.

'Not seen you here before.'

'Just passing through.'

Now he looked at me more closely, checking I wasn't some undercover poet who would jump up on the stage with a broken bottle in his hand.

'Banjo?'

'Ukulele.'

'That's what I meant.' He checked his list of players. 'Be about half an hour. Three songs. No filth.'

Maybe I was being over-anxious and this was a friendly neighbourhood bar. The other acts weren't being jeered at or anything. A singer-songwriter was first up, and she sang with such a look of pain you knew she had spent weeks carefully crafting each line of each lyric. Unfortunately the sound system made her echo like a station announcer.

Next came a lad who sang Springsteen songs with a bitterness that made his position clear: 'If only I had come from a broken home and my dad had gone to prison and I'd been bullied at school instead of being brought up in a liberal middle-class south-coast suburb with a Neighbourhood Watch sticker in the window, then I too could write songs like this.'

A man in a 'Don't tase me bro' T-shirt played a Radiohead song. 'He always plays Radiohead,' moaned the woman sitting opposite me. 'They all play Radiohead. If I ran an open mic, I'd ban Radiohead.'

'I like him,' I said, but I liked him simply because he was even older than I was.

Then Johno played. He knew what the audience wanted and he knew they wanted it loud. He cranked up the volume and a police car slowed outside. The officer looked in, waved at someone and moved on. I realized then that this was an entirely local do: the small audience, the musicians, the police, everyone knew everyone else. They came here every week and heard the same songs from the same acts, and that was the way they liked it.

'Are we ready for something a bit different?' called out Johno.

No one was going to commit themselves to that.

'We got a newcomer … with a mandolin.'

Many times that day I had thought to myself: what you're doing is absurd – as I was packing my bags; while I was waiting for the train; as I walked along the Brighton seafront; and now, as I stepped up to the microphone at the Three Graces.

There was no need for me to be here – this wasn't community service or anything. Nor was there any money involved. I was here voluntarily. I had told myself that a nationwide tour of open mics would be an original way to travel the country; it would allow me to feel the nation's musical pulse; it would be the rock 'n' roll tour I never had.

It would also be fun. That's what I told myself.

The audience seemed suddenly very quiet. I took a swig of water and had my first experience of the moment I would have every night over the next six weeks, the moment when I thought: this could go really well – or really badly.

I said, 'Hello Brighton.'

'This is Hove, mate,' someone called back.

'Oh, is it? Hello Hove then … right … Chuck Berry song.'

I launched into 'Roll Over Beethoven', and it was as if I had thrown myself off Beachy Head, just hoping that someone would be there at the bottom to catch me.

What do you do when your kids leave home? You can pine and look at old photos. You can say 'good luck' and rent out the extra space. Way down the list comes: pick up your ukulele and hit the road. But in the end it was the only thing I could do.

Music had played a huge part in my boys' upbringing. It was how we all got through the teenage years. I watched them grow up learning to play; I encouraged them to practise; I became their roadie as they joined bands. I felt proud as they gave concerts, tearful as they won prizes. It was when they went off on a tour of Greece with the school jazz band that I realized I also felt envious.

Music gave them so much fun, the sort of fun we should all have in our lives. When they left home, everyone imagined I would feel bereft, and part of me did, but most of me thought: okay, now it's my turn.

I had one problem: I couldn't play an instrument. But that was about to change.

It was my birthday shortly before they left and their gift to me was a ukulele. I strummed it happily, then, after they'd gone, put it back in the box and on top of the wardrobe.

Ukulele? I had more ambitious plans. I was about to start classical guitar lessons.

Like many young men looking for ways to impress women, I'd tried to teach myself guitar as a teenager. I spent a long time sitting on the edge of the bed clumsily playing 'The Sound Of Silence' with the window open in the hope that someone would sleep with me or discover me – either would do.

Learning classical guitar was a different challenge. It involved reading music; posture was important, so was growing my fingernails and filing them to an elegant curve. I took it all very seriously. I worked at Fernando Sor studies. I bought a nail maintenance kit from Boots. I practised every evening, and even considered a chart with stars on. Eventually my teacher decided I was ready for an exam.

As I walked into the room the examiner looked at me as if to ask, was I lost? I convinced him I was a more mature student, and then proceeded to play my pieces as if I had dementia. Somehow I passed and I proudly stuck my certificate on the wall next to my children's. I knew I wasn't fooling anyone, though. My plan was to reach Grade 8, but at the rate I was going I'd be 85 years old by that time; the examiner would have to help me up out of the chair. If my musical career was going to get off the ground, I needed to reconsider my options. I decided the best thing to do was join a grumpy old man's rhythm and blues band.

It was actually remarkably easy to do this. A friend wanted some live music for his wedding. Five of us volunteered with an alacrity that each hoped would appear nonchalant, but was plainly a lunge at the one and only chance to be in a band any of us had ever had.

We were a sad outfit: a lead guitarist who had never played outside his attic; a bass player whose musical influences included Trotsky; a drummer who surrounded himself with a full kit, but only ever hit one drum; a keyboard player who defaulted to Chopin if ever he got lost; and on vocals and rhythm guitar, yours truly, a frontman with a tendency to poke himself in the eye with the microphone whenever he stepped up to sing.

But we had two things in common: a love of rhythm and blues and no idea how to play it. We called ourselves the Elderly Brothers.

'That's a joke name,' I said to the bass player.

'Be honest, we're a joke band.'

We all had the same plan: to hide behind the others. And we managed to pull it off, to a point. The wedding was a triumph, if you ignored the guest who said we were the worst band he had ever heard and he was going to sit in his car. ('We'll put that on the debut CD,' said our drummer.) From there we went on to hide behind each other at a PTFA summer ball, a hang-gliding club's AGM, and a silver wedding anniversary when the proper band couldn't make it. These were halcyon days. We were five guys with three chords, the stars of Fiona the yoga teacher's 50th birthday party.

But then we blew it. We were asked to headline at the vicar's retirement do. It was a prestige gig and a step too far. Halfway through our performance a piece of women's underwear was thrown on the stage. It lay there, grey and industrial. We all looked at it and didn't know what to do – there was nothing in the manual about this. We played the rest of the set with an unclaimed brassiere lying on the stage. It was the day the music died.

I went home and lay on my bed, contemplating the awful truth that I might not have a musical future. That was when my eyes fell on the ukulele on top of the wardrobe.

The great thing about the ukulele – and you have to understand this before you start to play one – is it's supposed to sound a bit rubbish. A rough approximation is what you're after. You've only got four strings, for heaven's sake.

And yet it's cool! The association with George Formby and cleaning windows is no longer valid. Now punk bands use ukuleles. So do reggae bands, dubstep, blues. Ukuleles are all-purpose, and so easy to play that schools are starting to use them in place of the recorder. It didn't take long for me to realize here was the instrument I'd been looking for all my life.

Songs that would have taken me forever to learn on the guitar I could bash out on my uke with ease. Within a few weeks I made my debut at a fund-raiser for a new school bottle bank. This was followed by a performance at a New Year's Eve village talent show in which I came third behind a drag act and a Norman Wisdom impersonator. It wasn't quality, but it was delivered with purpose. I'm pleased to say that success went to my head. After two months I had 20 minutes of material. After three I was ready for the road.

What is it about the rock 'n' roll tour that fires the imagination so? Any musician who has been on one likes to be blasé and tell you they are the most demoralizing, uncomfortable, boring, near-death experiences they've ever had. Which sounds just fine to the rest of us. The urge to trash a hotel room is a primal one. The Elderly Brothers were so desperate to go on the road, we once considered a tour of local nursing homes.

But the Elderly Brothers couldn't have toured. Our keyboard player liked to be in bed by 11 o'clock, and there wouldn't have been enough room in the van for our lead guitarist to put all his kit in. A solo ukulele tour, however, was a very different prospect. Here was an instrument I could wrap in a T-shirt and put in a backpack. I could be completely independent. The moment I saw myself as a wandering minstrel – arriving in town, giving a concert and moving on – I was hooked. All I was missing was somewhere to play.

I thought about busking, but the ukulele wasn't loud enough for the street. A tour of ukulele clubs? Didn't really get the adrenalin going. What I needed was an open platform, a place I could visit in every town where anyone could get up and perform just for fun. I didn't know it, but there were hundreds of them all over the country.

I was driving home one evening when I saw a sign outside a pub: *Open Mic, Tuesday. All Welcome.* I went and sat through some dull stuff for half an hour, mostly people thrashing away at guitars, but then a diamond took the stage, a teenager who could play her instrument, and sang as though her life depended on it. Then a fast and furious poet stepped up. Then a drunk who sang a folk song unaccompanied and everyone politely applauded. As the place filled up, a three-piece band took over and fumbled their way to closing time.

Some of it was good, a lot of it was awful, but the beauty of it was it was entirely democratic. Anyone of any age or ability could get up and have their three songs' worth. They just needed the bottle to do it. It was like the unedited, unairbrushed version of *Britain's Got Talent*, and the rubbish was as important as the pick. I reckoned I could get away with it.

I went online and randomly Googled 'open mics'. Bristol, Newcastle, Edinburgh – they were full of them. In York I counted four on a Thursday night alone. There were also websites that listed open mics in any given area. And they weren't just in cities. A country pub might have one every third Tuesday. Village halls held them, so did arts centres. I phoned a few to check the advertised nights were still running, and although half of them weren't, I suspected there were as many again that didn't have websites, that just put a sign outside, or a note on Facebook. It would be hit and miss, but I was sure there were more than enough for an extensive tour.

All I needed was a start and finish point. I liked the idea of beginning on the south coast and working my way north. Brighton offered a number of choices and would be a good place to kick off. From there I could head west and up towards Bristol, maybe into Wales, through the North and into Scotland. How far could I go? I searched for the most remote open mic in Britain. I found it at the Smoo Cave Hotel right by Cape Wrath.

'No. We don't have an open mic,' the manager said when I called. Was that the sea I could hear crashing on a rocky shore and the lighthouse fog horn blaring in the distance?

'It's advertised on the Durness community website,' I said.

'We've never had an open mic. But I'll tell you what: if you can get here, you can play all you want.'

That sounded like a challenge. It also sounded as though she was offering me the chance to play a concert, not just a three-song cameo. I hesitated. Was I really up to a concert? I'd have to get an act together. I'd need patter. I'd need an encore! I closed my eyes and saw myself tramping up the country, through sun and rain, being ignored in the south, laughed at in the west, but then making them start to take notice in the Midlands, getting them to sing along in the North, playing to packed houses in the Lowlands, and then coming over a pass and seeing the Smoo Cave Hotel right on the cliff edge at Cape Wrath and there, in the window, a poster: *Tonight. One performance only. The Uke of Wallington.*

'I'll do it,' I said.

She gave me a date six weeks after my start day. Six weeks on the road to get myself into shape.

If I'd had a day job, I would have given it up right there.

'A concert?!' said my wife.

'Why not?'

She didn't want to tell me the truth. 'In front of people you don't know?'

'My plan is to improve as I go along.'

'You don't think this is a young man's activity?'

'Bob Dylan is 70.'

'Bob Dylan started playing when he was a teenager.'

'So did I.'

She could see she wasn't going to get anywhere down this track. She said, 'It's hard when the children leave. You're bound to feel at a loss.'

'I'm not at a loss. A rock 'n' roll tour is something I've always wanted to do.'

'How can you do rock 'n' roll on a ukulele?'

'I'll show you.'

'No it's all right … I believe you.'

'You think it's a mid-life crisis, don't you?'

'No. You're too old for a mid-life crisis.'

Transport? A tour bus of course. Every rock 'n' roll tour needed a tour bus. Since I was solo maybe a camper van. Since I didn't have a camper van, maybe my beat-up Ford Fiesta.

But cars are a nuisance on a trip like this. I preferred the wandering minstrel image, carrying everything on my back. I'd travel on foot, and take public transport when needed. I would have a tour bus: it would be the next bus that came along.

I put a set list together, songs that above all I liked to sing: Chuck Berry, Dave Edmunds, Chuck Berry. Any good rhythm and blues. I was aware this wasn't the sort of material you normally heard on the ukulele, but it was lively, and made an audience sit up. Finally I learnt to play 'Happy Birthday'. You never know when you might need to play 'Happy Birthday'.

I rehearsed long and hard, so long and hard I realized I was missing something. My ukulele was purely rhythm. When it came to the instrumental breaks in the songs, all I could offer was more of the same plinky plonky stuff.

Something was needed that would give that all-important lift in the middle. I tried the mouth organ – far too difficult. I tried whistling – made me sound like Jiminy Cricket. There was only one instrument that would do, the one patented by Warren Herbert Frost in 1883. The kazoo.

With pliers and fuse wire I twisted a coat hanger into a custom-made brace. I fixed my plastic yellow kazoo in place and played 'Jailhouse Rock'. When the time came for the guitar solo, I improvised on the kazoo. The dog started to bark.

I played it again and this time watched myself in the hallway mirror. It was either brilliant or dreadful and I didn't want to know which.

I packed the bare essentials: ukulele, sleeping bag and, by far the best invention for the light-weight traveller, trousers that unzipped at the knees and became shorts.

My wife was also packing. She had decided to cope

with my absence by going to Italy with a friend.

'That's very resourceful of you,' I said.

'It's the sort of thing normal people do with their summer holiday.'

The night before we both left I played her three songs, making her promise not to say anything in any way critical. She listened politely and then afterwards sat there with a smile.

'Why are you smiling?'

'You told me not to say anything.'

'The smile means something.'

'You're right.'

'What?'

'I can't tell you.'

'Yes, you can.'

'It means … that whenever you hear a ukulele it makes you smile.'

That was a very interesting theory, one I was going to test to the limit over the coming weeks.

In the end the Three Graces gig didn't go too badly. I didn't get a standing ovation and I didn't get abuse, which was good because I couldn't have coped with either. What I wanted on this first night was indifference – I could build on indifference – and that was pretty much what I got.

I remember concentrating very hard. I probably had the look of a man performing organ transplant surgery rather than a song on a ukulele. As I played the kazoo solo I glanced up and the expression on faces was mixed.

Some were laughing. Some had a look that said, 'I would rather be home watching *Question Time.*' Some were thinking, 'I could do that.'

They had the relaxed look of an audience who had seen it all. I played a Nick Lowe song next and forgot the lyrics a couple of times and messed up the chord changes, but when I looked up half of them were playing with their phones. I tried to say something funny. 'Thanks for bearing with me as I go through my ukulele and kazoo phase.' But no one could have cared less.

To finish I played 'Route 66' about as ruggedly as you can on a ukulele. Someone sang 'Get your kicks on route 66' at every chorus, which was nice and supportive, and then that was that.

'Thank you very much, you've been a wonderful audience.' I meant it. Thanks to them I wouldn't be going straight back home.

'Can I ask you something?' a woman said to me later.

'Sure.'

'Is that a coat hanger round your neck?'

'Yes.'

'Thought so.'

As I left I said to Johno, 'Why no poets?'

He sighed. 'Poets just … spoil everything.'

This was a new and strange world to me, but I would get used to it. I slung my uke over my shoulder and strode off down the road. No after-show party, no press interviews. I could have gone home and thrown a TV out of the window, but the friends I was staying with would've looked pretty poorly on that.

Besides, I was too busy enjoying the thrill of having got up on stage in front of a bunch of strangers and not entirely humiliated myself. The tour had begun. Next stop, Worthing. How rock 'n' roll was that?

the isle of wight festival

The Brighton seafront was its own stage the following day as I walked off down the coast. A saxophonist was working his way through jazz standards. I felt a camaraderie with him and put 50p in his hat. I felt a camaraderie with the African drummer a hundred yards further down and put 50p in his hat as well. I could only afford 30p-worth of camaraderie with the accordion player who came next, and by the time I reached the heavy metal guitarist with his amp plugged into a car battery, my camaraderie was down to 10p and a nod of support.

I wanted all the good karma I could get. Having survived the previous evening, I had hoped to feel more at ease, but I was aware that in eight hours I'd be back at the mercy of an audience, and it didn't take much for me to start questioning the sanity of the whole project all over again.

I needed to distract myself, and that was easy walking down this front. It was a beautiful sunny day, the ice cream kiosks were doing good business and Brighton was trying its best to look like Nice, although that can be a struggle when your promenade is lined with municipal beach huts. It was all so effortlessly British. A woman sat in a deckchair and painted her toenails. Her husband did the crossword with the paper resting on his big belly. In the background was the sound of waves on shingle and the radio tennis commentary from Wimbledon where Andy Murray had taken the lead against Nadal.

I walked to Portslade then picked up the first of my tour buses, the 700 Coastliner, which connected Brighton with Portsmouth. The driver seemed oddly unprepared when I offered him cash. I understood why when I climbed to the top deck and saw that every passenger was over 60 and the proud owner of a concessionary ticket.

I felt like I'd gatecrashed a party. These fit, suntanned pensioners climbed up the stairs with a sprightliness that only a free outing can give you. The minute they sat down they were tucking into picnics. One of them saw my backpack. 'On holiday?'

'Yes.'

'Have bus pass will travel, eh?'

It took me a moment to realize he imagined I had a pass too. I felt aggrieved. I was 58, damn it, not even 58 and a half yet. How could he possibly think I was 60?

'It's easy travelling round East Sussex,' he said. 'Plenty of buses. And plenty of public toilets if you get caught.' He offered me a mini Bakewell tart. 'They're after their "Best Before", but we don't worry about that.'

I took one, to show him I didn't mind living dangerously. As I leant over, my bag toppled off the seat and the protruding ukulele struck a woman on the leg. I'd covered the head with a woollen mitten, but she still yelped.

'Carol bruises very easily,' said her friend.

'What is that anyway?' Carol asked.

I didn't want to explain. But I couldn't think of anything else it might be. 'It's a ukulele.'

'He's got a ukulele.'

All her friends turned to look. I knew what was on their minds. I could see us all cruising down the coast singing 'Ukulele Lady'. I was saved by a man who had got down from the bus and tripped over the pavement. From the top deck they all got a good view. 'Poor love,' said one. 'That's how Pauline did her hip.'

I got off at Shoreham. The afternoon was hotter still and I put on some suncream. A man rode past on a mobility scooter. He laughed at me and said, 'You don't want that stuff. You want your vitamin D. We don't use that stuff down here.'

Who were these who people didn't care about 'Best Before' dates or melanomas? They'd given up worrying. They were behaving as if they'd all come to live in paradise, or the waiting room for paradise anyway.

Shoreham sparkled with the sun and the salt water. I crossed the harbour on a wooden footbridge to where a line of houseboats lay moored up the River Adur. They were all marooned in the mud, and their Bohemian, distressed glamour had turned them into an off-beat tourist attraction. Each boat was trying to be more alternative than its neighbour. One had incorporated the side of a bus into its hull; another advertised the opera it was hosting later in the month. Vegetables grew on deck and there was an air of carefully crafted hippydom. It all came at a cost though. A freehold on a mooring was advertised for £150,000. Then you had to buy a boat to put on it.

'Nowhere cheap round Shoreham,' said a man working on his hanging baskets. 'You pay a million for one of those houses on the seafront. Maybe not a million. Half a million. Bit more than that. Seven hundred and fifty.'

There were indeed some grand and designer houses by the beach, but no one looked more proud of their property than the beach hut owners. In Lancing a couple were sitting out in front of theirs. She was knitting what looked like a map of South America. He was listening to the tennis on the radio. On the table between them sat a fruitcake and a pot of tea with cosy. I asked how one went about acquiring a hut.

'You mean shed,' he said proudly. 'That's all it is. A shed. I bought it at B&Q and painted it up.'

'You can buy or rent from the council,' said his wife. 'Fellow up the row there paid five thousand for his.'

'I'd rather have my shed.'

'In Bournemouth I've heard you can pay eight thousand.'

'Bournemouth,' he muttered. 'I'd rather be here than Bournemouth.'

You could see why. With Lancing College in the distance looking medieval through the heat haze, and vintage aircraft taking off from Shoreham airfield just over the road, there was something very Battle of Britain about the whole scene.

'Did Andy Murray win?' I asked.

'He lost.'

Made you proud to be British.

Hells Angels don't die; they just buy a mobility scooter and move to Worthing. There they zip down the pavements scattering pedestrians as lawlessly as they did in their prime.

There was a good trade in second-hand scooters all along the coast; dealers had them parked on their forecourts – *one lady owner*. In Worthing there was also a good business in stairlifts, power wheelchairs and the latest hearing technology. The grey pound ruled, which made me wonder what sort of audience I'd have at the open mic that evening in Barney's Bar. Maybe it would be a night of Vera Lynn and Frank Sinatra songs, although my guess was that the streets would be deserted by 8.30 and all residents tucked up in bed with the electric blanket on.

I was underestimating the local youth. The minute the last scooter was back home on charge, out stepped the young people in numbers, the lads carrying beer bottles and being tribal, the girls tottering on high heels and leaving a trail of perfume.

I was staying with my friend Colin who lived nearby. He'd spent many years as a street performer all over Europe. 'You can give me some tips,' I said.

'I will.'

'How to work an audience.'

'It's a piece of cake.'

Barney's Bar looked more like a piece of trouble. There was security on the door for a start – two smart dudes in black suits and shirts, each clutching a bottle of mineral water like a weapon.

'What's in the bag?'

'Ukulele.'

I thought he was going to break it over my head for being cheeky, but the other one said, 'My dad plays the ukulele.'

'What, when he's cleaning windows?' said his mate.

They laughed and parted just enough for Colin and me to squeeze between them.

Barney's wasn't the sort of place I would have expected to find an open mic. It was all chrome and strip lighting, and there was a more trendy, disco crowd than the previous evening. It was a pick-up joint and I missed the homeyness of the Three Graces. I even missed the homeyness of the 700 bus. This place looked sharp and competitive. There was a young woman already on stage with a voice like Shirley Bassey, belting out torch songs, showing off her tonsils, literally reaching out to the audience. Next to her on a stool sat a jaded guitarist. He was trying to keep up with her, but not trying that hard. She didn't care. She closed her eyes and she was in Las Vegas, wearing a million-dollar frock with Oscar Peterson accompanying her. 'I'll just do one more,' she said at the end of every song before anyone could tell her to stop and let someone else have a go.

There was a good number of performers waiting, a much

longer list than in Brighton. We had a drink and waited as the place began to fill up. The clientele got younger as the performers got older. A guitarist with a grey mop-top sang some Beatles tunes, including an acrobatic version of 'A Day In The Life'. He was good, but I couldn't stop wondering whether he qualified for a bus pass.

'If they put stuff like that on the telly …' said the woman next to me, but I didn't hear how she finished the sentence, whether she would have welcomed it or switched off.

Two lads sang a Radiohead song. The vocalist had his phone cupped in his hand around the microphone and was reading the lyrics.

'Do you do any Radiohead?' said Colin.

'No.'

'Maybe you should.'

But then the next act got up and they, too, sang Radiohead. Radiohead songs were open-mic fodder; they were what teenagers played in their bedrooms these days, the way previous generations had played The Smiths and Simon and Garfunkel.

'I used to like Radiohead,' said the woman next to me, 'but …' It wasn't that I didn't hear the end of her sentences, it was that she didn't finish them.

The host gave me the nod. I was on next, just as a stag party arrived and filled the place with a bovine bellowing. I said to Colin, 'What am I supposed to do with a mob like this?'

He nodded, wisely. 'This reminds me of the time I was juggling on the north coast of Spain. I had a similar crowd on a hot summer's night.'

'What did you do?'

'I bombed.'

'Great.'

'The only time I got their attention was when I fell off my unicycle.'

I walked calmly to the microphone. 'Good evening.'

One person turned round and regarded me like a fly he wanted to swat.

I struck a chord, forcefully. A few heads turned but turned away again having seen nothing. Maybe I was so anxious I'd become invisible. I struck the chord again, closed my eyes and sang as loudly as I could 'You ain't nothin' but a hound dog'. When I opened them, a large woman with dyed blonde hair and too much make-up was walking right past me.

I put my head down and played my three songs, getting faster and faster. I didn't give them time not to applaud. Afterwards I shoved my uke back in its bag and we would have left by the back door had there been one. The woman next to me said, 'Have you got a girlfriend?'

'No, I haven't.'

'If I was your girlfriend I'd ...'

I didn't hear the end of her sentence, not because she didn't finish it, but because I was already out on the street.

'That was very brave,' said Colin as we walked back through town.

'Thanks.'

'I wouldn't worry about it.'

'I'm not.'

'I mean, don't go letting it get you down or anything.'

'I wasn't.'

'There'll be loads of nights like that.'

For all its daytime gentility, Friday night in Worthing had turned into a scene from *Gladiator*. Cars drove round like chariots with people hanging out of them. Youths ran round roaring and throwing half-eaten kebabs across the street. I saw a queue of people waiting to get into a church, which seemed unlikely, but then I realized the church was a bar and disco.

On the opposite pavement stood a small group dressed like traffic wardens. I dismissed them as a fancy dress party, but then I realized they were a squad of some sort. They were all wearing badges that said 'Street Pastor'.

'We're here to help people,' one of them told me.

'Who?'

'People who might be drunk or over-emotional.'

'And women whose stiletto heels have broken, for example,' said his colleague with a smile like an air stewardess. 'I've got a pair of flip-flops in my bag. Just in case.'

They were church members. They said they wanted to reach out to the youth and 'discuss what influences their life choices'. And I thought I had a tough audience that night.

We drove back to Colin's house. 'So, any tips?' I said.

'No, you were fine.'

'You can be honest.'

'You could do something about your stage presence.'

'Meaning?'

'Wear a hat, or a bow tie, or a sparkly shirt. At the moment you look like you've just come in from the garden.'

The town had returned to normal next morning. At the bus stop there was a familiar line of senior citizens. 'We normally have to wait until 9.30,' said one. She meant off-peak time, when concessions started to operate, but it was Saturday so they could get an early start.

'Where are you going?' I said.

'Ooh, don't ask.'

'Why not?'

'We're off to Littlehampton for coffee.'

Life was good with a bus pass, there was no doubt. I wanted one after all. I wondered whether there was a market in fake ones, like the IDs all the underage kids had bought drinks with the previous night.

The Coastliner scooped us up and carried on heading westward through Goring and Durrington-on-Sea. They were sitcom place names – Captain Mainwaring country – and appeared to be one long line of kit-built development thrown up in the 1930s. The streets were spotless. Dog owners walked their little darlings with retractable lead in one hand and plastic bag in the other. The dog poo didn't hit the floor. It was caught mid-air in the bag and dropped into one of the many designated receptacles. It was little wonder that the young people came out at night and tried to mess the place up a bit.

At Littlehampton there was a sandy beach at last, and a natural harbour on the River Arun. I sat on a bench and unzipped the knees of my trousers. People looked round when they heard a zipping noise and regarded me disapprovingly. Maybe this was something that needed to be done in private.

Littlehampton inspired me to take my first photograph of the trip, of the ornate bollards along the harbour inscribed with fish recipes. Grilled plaice – *brush fish with butter, and grill on both sides until golden brown*. It was a bit lame really, not much of a way to remember a lost fishing industry. If you were going to put up plaques, then I thought you had to celebrate the people who came from the town. A quick piece of research on my phone told me that the only famous locals were The Body Shop's Anita Roddick and a particularly nasty child murderer. Baked stuffed bass – *pack fish with stuffing, bake for 30 mins.*

I mooched around these little towns like a panting dog, looking for shade, drinking water at any tap. In Bognor where Butlins loomed over the town like an institution I wandered onto the pier, curious to see the point where the Birdmen of Bognor jumped off once a year in a wonderfully mad seaside competition that saw crackpot aviators attempt to propel themselves a very ambitious 100 metres.

In 2009 everyone thought Steve Elkins had done it, and he claimed the £30,000 prize. But officials logged his flight at 99.88 metres and the prize money was withheld. There were strong protests, but it seemed to me a display of exactitude and inflexibility completely in keeping with West Sussex. This county didn't get where it was today by ignoring 0.12 of a metre.

A man sat on the pier in a hat and coat, reading a newspaper with the headline: *Hottest Weekend of the Year*. He said to me, 'Bognor Regis is the best place to live in the world.'

'Where else have you lived?'

'Basildon.'

Chichester Cathedral was visible from the top deck of the bus from miles away. It's the only cathedral in England visible from the sea. Sailors used to look out for the spire as a landmark.

The two young lovers on the front seat weren't bothered. They snogged the whole journey from Bognor. Behind them an elderly man tried to distract himself. He said to his wife, 'Look down there, grey mullet.'

We were crossing a river and there were big, lumpy fish swimming round in circles by the bridge supports.

'What about them?' she said.

'You can eat them.'

She wasn't interested. She was laden with jewellery, and tanned and wrinkled to the shade of a dried tobacco leaf. Her husband had persuaded her to travel by bus because it was free, but he wasn't going to get her to eat anything as ugly as grey mullet.

The youngsters fondled each other and giggled. The man tried to look away again. 'They taste a bit muddy that's all.'

'What?'

'Grey mullet.'

He wasn't helping to change her mind. 'We should eat more fish at our age,' he said. 'Good for the heart.' He put his bony arm through hers and she smiled her special smile for him as the two in front rolled over the seat.

Grey mullet, the fish of romance.

Inside Chichester Cathedral it was cool and restful, but not quiet. There was a stage with an elaborate sound and lighting setup. A sound check was in progress for a concert that evening by a band called Blake. They were four young men, a sort of classical boy band, and they ran effortlessly through 'Wild Mountain Thyme' and then 'Ave Maria', before one of them waved things to a stop. It didn't sound right, he said. It didn't sound the way it had in Norwich.

'You mean Ely,' said his bandmate.

'Yeah. Ely.'

What was this: a tour of cathedrals? They looked saintly enough, so well groomed and well trained, like grown-up choir boys. I wondered how they'd go down at Barney's Bar. They had a much better engineer on the mixing desk, that was for sure. It may not have sounded as good as it did in Ely, but it sounded impressive enough in this huge space. I debated whether to stay for the evening and hear the concert, but then they put me off by rehearsing a Radiohead song.

I had nowhere to play that night – there was never an open mic on a Saturday – but there was one the following evening in Sandown on the Isle of Wight, and so when the

Coastliner finally deposited me at Portsmouth Harbour and turned back, I caught the ferry over to Ryde. I found a guesthouse and got a bicycle, and spent the rest of the weekend cycling round the island. It was all a bit out of my way, but I had wanted to come to the Isle of Wight. I had unfinished business here.

There were boats everywhere you looked: the sea fluttered with yachts, so did every river and lagoon. Houseboats were hauled up on shingle beaches; freighters anchored out in the Solent, and tankers off the channel coast. And there were the ferries, of course. The island depended on its ferries that barged their way across the Solent, with sailing boats and motor launches zipping around their huge hulls like wind-up bath toys.

I cycled west along the Tennyson Trail, a high chalky track that followed the ridge of the Downs, giving wonderful views. Tennyson lived on the island for 40 years and used to walk up here, saying that the air was worth sixpence a pint. But it wasn't his connection with the island that had brought me here. It was a man who let his guitar speak for him – Jimi Hendrix.

From the top of the Downs you could look west across Poole Bay over to Dorset where the same chalk ridge surfaced once more in Swanage. It was in this little resort on the Isle of Purbeck that I lived as an awkward 17-year-old in 1970 when it was announced that Jimi Hendrix was to play at the Isle of Wight Festival. I immediately made plans to go with a group of friends, but there was a problem. I had a job in a pie and chip shop that was open all hours through the season and when I asked to take the bank holiday weekend off my request was, perhaps understandably, met with a flat refusal. Any self-respecting 17-year-old would have untied his apron and walked out, but I was too well behaved and told my friends I couldn't go.

And so I managed to missed the biggest pop festival there has ever been. A reported 600,000 people found their way over to the Isle of Wight that weekend. The population of the island trebled. The local council, reacting to resident groups who wanted these undesirable visitors nowhere near them, shunted the festival as far to the west as possible, to East Afton Farm near Freshwater Bay. This just meant that everyone had to trudge right across the island to get there.

Hippies weren't known for their respect for property. They were known more for eating anything they could find, and the fine vegetable patches of Cowes and all places west were undoubtedly looted. Nudity and drugs provoked the more reactionary islanders even further. All this, added to the sheer scale of the event, and the fact that it was Hendrix's last big concert before he died, has made sure Isle of Wight 1970 is still one of the most talked about festivals of them all.

And all the time I was serving pie and chips. I would come out to empty the bins and look across the water to The Needles and know I was missing out on something formative. I don't think I ever properly got over it. I went to many other festivals as a teenager, but still the one I remember the most is the one I missed. Forty years later I was looking for closure.

I headed along the ridge towards Freshwater Bay, past Tennyson's monument, until I came to the golf course and there was East Afton Down. I recognized the view immediately from pictures. It was unspoilt farmland now, but over that weekend 40 years ago, a multitude stretched down the slope to a tiny stage where the biggest names in rock music had gathered. The hillside meant that those who didn't want to pay didn't have to. They just sat on the side of the Downs and could easily see over the whole site. The fence was soon knocked down anyway so that halfway through the weekend the organizers declared it a free festival. No profit was made, and that, as much as the residents' reaction, meant that it would be the last Isle of Wight Festival until 2002.

Hendrix finally played his set in the early hours of the Monday morning. It was beset by technical problems and by all accounts he didn't put on much of a show. Joni Mitchell and The Who seem to figure larger in most memories; and one other, rather more unlikely performer, Tiny Tim, who came on stage with his ukulele and, after asking everyone to show some respect and not laugh at him, played 'Tiptoe Through The Tulips', followed by 'There'll Always Be An England' (sung through a megaphone). Ukulele historians like to trace the resurgence of the instrument back to that appearance.

When you think of all the tourist information plaques that appear around the country, marking lost industries and long-forgotten people, when you see a town celebrating its heritage with fish recipes, you'd think something could have been put up here on Tennyson

Down to mark the site of such a memorable event. But it was as if the local council and islanders wanted to forget the whole occasion. The only memorial I could find was down in Freshwater Bay, at Dimbola Lodge, which is now a museum dedicated to the pioneer photographer Julia Margaret Cameron, and in the café garden there's a bronze statue of Hendrix.

The figure is scaled down and he looks young and frail, but he's clutching his guitar – left-handed, the tuning keys pointing down – and he's looking away at the beautiful white cliffs of the bay and the Downs. A lost soul.

As I left I walked back up the hill and came across a much older memorial on the cliff, one erected to a teenager who died accidentally in a fall in 1846. The plaque read: 'He cometh forth like a flower and is cut down. He fleeth also as a shadow and continueth not ... Reader prepare to meet thy God, for thou knowest not what a day may bring forth.'

It's unlikely Hendrix went for a walk on the Downs and read this the weekend he was here, and that's a shame. Three weeks after the festival ended the accidental death was his own.

A disused railway line had been turned into a cycle track and it led me lazily down from Newport towards Sandown, through golden fields of grain waving in the breeze in classic fashion. *Look out for grey wagtails*, a sign told me, which is all very well if you know what one looks like.

I'd had another day of distractions, but the nearer I got to Sandown the more my stomach tightened again. Once more that evening I had to climb up on a stage and sing to a room full of strangers. When I found the Sandown Tap it did little to encourage me. It had sounded almost exotic back at home when I was planning my route, but here it was, a pub offering two meals for a tenner and a television on every wall showing Sky Sports.

I checked the open mic was on. 'Gets going about eight,' said the barman.

'You get many people?'

'Gets packed.'

I didn't believe him. After the handsome Downs and the yacht club preppiness of the rest of the island, Sandown looked tired and empty. The first B&B I asked at grabbed me and pulled me inside. She asked me for money before I'd had a chance to put my bag down. 'Makes it easier,' she said. 'Get it over and done with now.'

'Can I pay by cheque?'

She backed away.

'Card?'

'There's a cash machine in the Co-op.'

I went and got cash for her and she took me down the side of the house to a room that smelt of sprouts.

Down on the beach front the souvenir shops were pulling down their shutters for the night. I managed to buy some faded postcards for 10p each. I said to the shop owner, 'Busy?'

'World War II weekend.'

'What happens?'

'Spitfires flying over, actors going round dressed like spivs. It was wonderful.'

'I missed it.'

'You can come next time. It's just nostalgia and stuff. Same every year.'

There was something about the Isle of Wight that seemed locked in nostalgia. A spitfire flying over or spivs offering nylons wouldn't have seemed out of place.

I went back to the Tap at eight o'clock as instructed. The open mic had started, although the TVs hadn't been turned off, just muted. There was a blues band playing, but there were so many screens flashing around the room it was hard to keep your eye on anything except the golf from Atlanta.

Pete, the band's singer, was hosting the evening and when they took a break I asked him to put me on the list. 'Sure. We're all really hammered, been at a stag do all day.'

Hammered they may have been, but they sounded good, and I liked the fact their bass player was well over the age of 70.

I sat at a table with a teenager and a grandma who had been on the World War II weekend. 'They re-created an air raid,' said the grandma. 'There was an ambulance and everything.'

'There was blood everywhere,' said the teenager.

'Fake blood,' said grandma.

'Kids today don't know what it was like,' said the teenager. 'They've no idea. They've got too many toys.'

She took her grandma out to the street for a smoke. On the TV a golfer in orange trousers sliced his ball into a sand trap. On the stage a woman in a long purple tie-dye dress slung a red electric guitar over her shoulder and said, 'I'm just going to play a few of my own songs.' She had an American accent and long grey hair, and with her tie-dye she looked as though she'd arrived for the festival all those years ago and never left.

A man with a violin sat next to me. He'd been at the stag do all day as well. He put his face too close to mine and said, 'What's that in your bag?'

'Ukulele.'

'Oh, I love a ukulele. What people don't appreciate about the ukulele is it's easy to play but very difficult to spell.'

A young woman who had been sitting on the knee of her sunburnt boyfriend got up next and performed with the house band. She sang like Janis Joplin and had a local fanbase who gathered at the foot of the stage and took pictures of her on their phones. Her boyfriend tried to act like security, although it was hard to take him seriously with his red, peeling nose.

She was only a teenager and she may as well have worn a T-shirt that said, 'I Need to Get Off This Island Before I Die of Boredom'. As soon as she finished her songs, her boyfriend whisked her out as if there was a limo waiting for her, and all her fans left with her. The remaining audience numbered about six, and now it was my turn.

The drunk violinist gave me a loud round of applause. 'Oh, I love a ukulele!' It was tough going though. I played a Buddy Holly song as an opener, and to be fair the audience all looked up, a few were even tapping their feet. But by the start of the second song, they were watching the golf. By the end of it, I was watching the golf myself.

I pressed on. I played Chuck Berry's 'Teenage Wedding' to see if I could derail them with a dance number. A whole table got up and went outside to have a smoke.

'And for my last song,' I said, and I told them how I had been to see the statue of Jimi Hendrix that day and, although I didn't know any Hendrix songs, I did know one by Big Bill Broonzy, which Rory Gallagher had played at the 1970 Festival.

It could have been the first time 'I Feel So Good' has ever been performed on ukulele and kazoo. I put a lot of effort into it, growled a bit. And, gradually, I thought I was winning them over. I definitely saw a man at the bar moving his left shoulder in time with the music. Another stopped and listened with his pint halfway to his mouth. But then the golf switched to motor racing and I lost them again. I found myself hurrying towards the end, even thinking of cutting the second kazoo solo. And then something remarkable happened.

The music lifted a level. I thought Pete had flicked a switch on the sound mixer, but it was more fundamental than that. The beat was heavier, the kind of sound that a ukulele is incapable of producing. And then I heard a snare drum, and when I looked around the drummer from the blues band was sitting behind his kit, and playing next to him the old bass player. Together they were driving my song along, and it felt as if a wave had picked me up.

'I feel so good,' I sang, and we were rolling. Now heads were looking away from the TV. What was this? A ukulele and kazoo-led blues band? That was something you didn't often see. The smokers came back in and started clapping a rhythm. The violinist played air-ukulele. When we finished I noticed even the barman was applauding.

We didn't stop to think – me and my band. We played a Blind Willie McTell song next, then Elmore James's 'It Hurts Me Too'. Some Chuck Berry after that; some Bo Diddley, and then finished with a Buddy Holly classic, 'That'll Be The Day'. The audience whooped and whistled. I held my uke above my head. The band shook hands with me. The barman paid me the highest compliment of all by turning off the TVs. Pete asked me to come back and play the following week. The drunk violin player put his arm round me and said, 'Stay where you are, I've chosen you to accompany me on my violin.'

I convinced him it wouldn't work. I didn't want to spoil things. That night I lay awake in my lodgings, listening to the hum of the freezer parked right outside my room, and feeling deeply satisfied. I had finally exorcised the pain of the 1970 Festival. I'd let it go.

From now on whenever I thought of the Isle of Wight, I wouldn't think of Hendrix and the pie and chip shop, I'd think of Sunday night at the Sandown Tap.

stonehenge rock

The beauty of the ukulele is that if you practise you will get better, but not that much better. No one ever sold their soul to the devil to improve their ukulele playing. Once the basics have been learnt you can stop there if you want, unless you feel the need to fingerpick a Bach prelude like that pale-looking bloke on YouTube who probably has no friends.

When I discovered this I was delighted because I've always had a difficult relationship with practising. When I was a child I had piano lessons from a man who smelt of booze, chain smoked and spent the lesson with his hand on my knee. This seemed normal. What I resented was the music he gave me to play, which I loathed so much that practising it would reduce me to a wailing wreck. Not long ago I found the book he taught me from at the bottom of the piano stool when I rescued it from my parents' house, and just the sight of the green cover made me want to go and crouch in the corner.

When I started to take classical guitar lessons I was determined it would be different. I put aside a set time for practice every day. I worked slowly and methodically. Now, not only did I like the music, I found myself attracted to very technical composers such as Carcassi who specialized in sober pieces with titles like *Etude VIII*. I practised them over and over until my wrists hurt. I experimented with dynamics, with different fingering. I became obsessed with perfecting them. I got to the point where practising made me worse not better. I ended up in a heap on the floor again.

Practice sessions for the Elderly Brothers were comparatively painless, but that was because the three hours we put aside were much more to do with setting up and taking down the equipment, and included lengthy discussions on the correct way to coil a cable. There was little point in us learning new material, since we had this innate ability to make anything new sound like everything else we did. No matter how original the song, if it went through our rehearsal crusher, it emerged as a square lump of noise. It was what defined us as a band.

So I didn't need to do any technical ukulele practice on this trip, but I did need to keep my repertoire in reasonable shape and gradually extend it. I was going to need a varied half-hour set by the time I got to Cape Wrath, which made it unhelpful to just play the same three songs over and over at open mics. Practising on the road wasn't easy though. It was hard to get any privacy, which was why I was sitting on a log in a water meadow along the River Itchen. I'd been following the path along the bank from Southampton to Winchester when I came across this pleasant spot where I couldn't see anyone and no one could see me, so I stopped and pulled out the uke.

Within a minute a black Labrador was sniffing at my feet. Then his owner appeared in shorts and wellington boots. If I came across someone in a field playing a ukulele I would give him a wide berth, but this man stood there with his hands in his pockets.

'Lovely day.'

'Lovely.'

'Ukulele, eh?'

'Yes.'

'I can't play the ukulele.'

His dog was taking a keen interest in my tuna and sweetcorn sandwich from Sainsbury's Local.

'Leave the man's lunch alone, Stanley.'

If Stanley ate my lunch there was a good chance I would have taken a bite out of Stanley.

'Do you know anything by Oasis?'

'No.'

'Dire Straits?'

'No.'

'Cliff Richard?'

'No.'

'How about "When I'm Cleaning Windows"?'

This was black Lab land. Dog walkers ruled the river bank, throwing sticks for their handsome animals who charged into the water then made everyone scream as they scrambled out and shook themselves. The owners were very strict. 'Harris! You've got your shirt dirty!' bawled a mother, not at her black Lab, but at her little lad who had scrambled down the bank after the dog. 'That's very bad. Straight to bed when we get home. No DVD for you.'

The Itchen was a beautiful chalk river, once a working navigation – Winchester's link with the sea – but now a lazy meandering course with swimming holes and little white beaches, which had been taken over by teenagers on another hot, hot day. Their exams were over and they lay in the sun, all pressure off now, a long, blissful summer ahead of them where nothing mattered. Until results day, that was. But that was ages away. The boys splashed the girls, and the girls shrieked and pouted, and I smiled when I thought of the same mating rituals being performed in these shady spots every summer since Alfred the Great took his A levels.

The river led me right into Winchester and to the immense cathedral. I could hear singing as I approached. Evensong. I hurried inside to catch a haunting choral piece, the voices reaching for the corners of the vast space. It was the end of the service, but I wanted to know what I'd heard and went to find the choir master.

'How *nice* to see you,' he said, shaking my hand. I was aware of myself standing there in shorts with red face and a mitten-topped ukulele sticking out of my bag, and yet this man seemed really happy to see me in his 1,000-year-old cathedral, and the fact that I wanted to know about his music was pure icing. 'It was Michael Tippett,' he told me. '"Deep River". Such a fun piece, isn't it?'

Fun wasn't a word I normally associated with Tippett's music, but this trip was already allowing me to see how tightly we all held on to our musical preferences. One man's Michael Tippett is another man's George Michael, as I discovered in a pub called the Railway later that evening.

The Railway was how I hoped open mics would be when I first thought of this trip: an upstairs room away from the main bar, with an audience who had come to listen, and someone on the sound desk who knew what they were doing.

There was even stage lighting, and this was clearly a well-established date in the local music diary because the room was full with all ages, and there was a long list of people wanting to play. The host wasn't convinced he could fit me in.

'It's not normally this busy,' he said. 'We've got a bunch of Americans.'

The Americans were the teenagers who had taken over one side of the room. They were an earnest group who were over here on a rock music course, the climax of which was a short tour of local open mics.

Across from them sat the regulars, trying their best not to appear put out. This sort of intrusion was hard enough to take, but it was also Independence Day and the Americans were in party mood. The odd thing was that despite a fortnight at what was clearly a very expensive summer school, they were out of their depth here. This was rich coming from me, I know, but even I could see these guys were under-rehearsed. When one of them played a Wham! song, the locals were watching through their fingers.

However, what the Americans lacked in performance skills they made up in audience participation. They thought everyone was wonderful and showed it. And, much as the locals disapproved of having their playing time cut, they clearly loved the response they got when they finally did get to play.

There was a good folk band, and then a singer in the Tracy Chapman style. There was even a poet who gave us a powerful 'State of the Nation' piece and received a rock star's reception from the Americans, who would have found 99 per cent of the references meaningless.

I didn't think I'd get the chance to play, but towards the end of the evening the host gave me the eye. 'Two songs. Make them short.'

I decided to play to the crowd. 'It's Independence Day! Let's hear some Chuck Berry.'

Call me a slut, I don't care. They loved it. They were clapping and singing along. They cheered the kazoo solo as if it was the most artistic thing they'd seen since they arrived in Britain. When I finished I thought: if there's ever a time on this trip to go crowd surfing this has to be it.

One more number. I thought: go on, play your Elvis. But I had my integrity, and I opted for a Nick Lowe song, which I hoped would convince the local half of the audience I wasn't entirely shameless.

The Americans gave the Nick Lowe the same ecstatic response as the Chuck Berry. Basically, I could have read out the cricket scores and they would have gone crazy.

Afterwards they all climbed into a bus and went back to base. The host said to me, 'Come back next week, it'll be back to normal.'

I quite liked it the way it was.

I got some practising in the next morning in the unlikely surroundings of the cathedral gardens. I'd gone there to wait until my bus left, and beneath the trees I found a man juggling, a woman doing gymnastics and a dog owner training his terrier to roll over, sit and beg. It was like a scene from a community education circus skills class, and a ukulele player was nothing extraordinary.

I was heading to Salisbury that day. I'd been to the library earlier to use a computer and found an open mic there that evening. I'd also discovered there was a footpath all the way from Winchester, the Clarendon Way. I just needed a bus to get me out of town.

The bus driver was very helpful. He told me the village of Broughton would be a good place to pick up the path. He said he'd call out when we got there. 'I'll write it down to remind myself, how's that?' After me, he assisted an elderly gent up the steps and guided him to his seat. Then he helped a woman with her shopping.

'You wouldn't get that in London,' said the woman opposite me.

'I've had him before,' said the man behind. 'He's very good.'

The driver turned round to us and said, 'We're about to leave, everyone ready?'

We all reported we were. The door hissed shut and he started the engine. He was breaking the speed limit before he left the terminus.

The next 45 minutes was a white-knuckle ride as he

swung that bus round country lanes at speeds I didn't think a bus could travel at. This wasn't how a drive through rural Hampshire was supposed to be, was it? I looked round at the other passengers for support – we could protest – only to realize they were the usual bus-pass brigade and that this, far from being an unsettling experience, was their daily thrill. They liked this bus driver because he gave them a roller-coaster ride home.

We plunged into a pothole and all the passengers rose up into the air. He slammed on the brakes and we were all flung forward. My neighbour was clinging on, the wind from the open window rushing through her hair. 'He's going to kill us all,' I wanted to say to her, but her response would have been, 'Yes, but what a way to go.'

We sped round a corner and there was a tractor coming straight at us. I closed my eyes and heard the crunching of vegetation against the window as we somehow managed to squeeze past.

'Bye now,' the driver said to me, as I climbed down in Broughton. 'See you again.'

I will always remember that man's face, and I will never see him again.

The hot, sunny spell had passed; rain began to fall as soon as I started walking. But I was just happy to be on foot. I dug out my waterproofs for the first time and headed off on the trail.

It was a chalk path and a white line had been worn in the earth, as if painted. I entered woodland. Rain dripped from the leaves; deer lifted their heads and trotted into the darkness of the trees. It just needed a wolf to leap out to complete the scene.

The woods gave way to a Roman road. Two women on horseback trotted up behind me. 'Enjoying your walk in the rain?' said one.

'We could give you a lift if you like?' said the other.

'Are you serious?' I said. I liked the idea of arriving in Salisbury on horseback, like a real wandering minstrel.

'Why not?' she said.

'Have you got insurance?' said her friend.

'Insurance for what?'

'Riding a horse.'

Of course I didn't have horse-riding insurance. I was a bloody troubadour. I'd abandoned stuff like insurance along with my pension plan.

'Can't risk it then, I'm afraid,' she said. 'Health and safety and all that. Sorry.' And they trotted away.

The Clarendon Way joined up with the Pilgrims' Way, then crossed the Monarch's Way and Sarum Way, which in turn led to the Orange Way and the Wessex Heights Walk. Paths ran through the countryside at all angles, all with some historical reference and a flowery name bestowed on them not by William of Orange or anyone who actually used the original trail, but by the relevant tourist board. Europeans just give their paths numbers, but we can't resist packaging them up. Tennyson had been given the ultimate branding, of course, on the Isle of Wight, with a 'way' named in his honour. Maybe in years to come my route would become known as the Minstrel's Way.

Middle-aged men with ukuleles would retrace my steps. The Tap in Sandown would have a plaque on the wall. A gunshot in the distance brought me back to reality.

I came to a clearing and the ruins of Clarendon Palace, a royal residence in the Middle Ages. As the information plaque quoting John Britten put it: 'The proud revellery of court has given way to the hooting of owls.' Or, in this case, the grazing of llamas. They wandered around the enclosure, looking even more dumb than sheep.

What the palace did still have intact was its fine view westward down the slope to the first glimpse of Salisbury Cathedral. The cloud was low but the needle of the spire pierced the gloom. My third cathedral in four days. This wasn't how I was expecting a rock 'n' roll tour to pan out, but the traveller is inexorably drawn to these colossal buildings, no matter how secular his business.

Quite apart from anything else, they were very good places to shelter in, from the sun in Chichester and Winchester, and in Salisbury from the cloud burst that greeted me on arrival. This time, I managed to get inside just as Evensong was starting. A clergyman directed me to a pew marked Ilfracombe, and I sat there in candlelight with the rain drumming on the roof.

A film crew was at work, making a documentary on the life of a chorister, we were informed. I was in a church choir as a child and all I could remember was singing 'Kyrie Eleison' over and over again with the occasional 'Credo in Unum Deum' thrown in. It wasn't a happy experience. We sang in fear of the raging choir master whose thread veins became so engorged if we made a mistake, he looked as though he might spontaneously combust. After I left, it was a long time before I was able appreciate choral music again.

Life as a Salisbury chorister seemed very different. They led a privileged life. Plucked out of the crowd aged seven, they received an education to be envied, and spent their days immersed in this glorious and historic music. No doubt they were told they were wonderful most of the time as well.

You could hear them before you could see them, coming in from the south transept, then turning in to the choir. They walked in procession, carrying candles, hair brushed neatly – no spikes or buzz cuts here. They filed into the stalls looking so innocent, so bubble-wrapped. The real world wouldn't kick in until their voices broke.

They sang a piece by Herbert Howells, which was so soothing that after a long day's hiking my head began to drop. But we kept having to stand up and sit down, stand up and sit down. My elderly neighbour was having a hard time of it all. He would manage to stagger to his feet only to be told to sit down again. 'Is it raining?' he said to me at one point. There had just been a lightning flash. 'I think it is,' I replied.

The thunder that followed made the great building groan. The congregation kept calm. If this was Judgement Day we were in the right place.

I walked hopelessly round the city through the rain, looking for somewhere to stay. Salisbury was a big player on the

British tour, as well as a base for visiting Stonehenge, and it was hard to find a cheap room. I got the last bed in town in a guesthouse that was beyond my budget. I rang the bell and a richly suntanned woman in an evening dress opened the door with a wide smile, which disappeared the minute she saw the damp muddy figure on the doorstep. One wet day was all it took to go from beach-boy to tramp.

I had a bath, did some laundry and lay on the bed, grumbling. I felt irritated because I'd just seen a notice that informed me a cooked breakfast was £5 extra. When Led Zeppelin drummer John Bonham had a grievance with a hotel during a tour, the story goes he rode a motorbike down the corridor to make his point. Keith Moon used to set fire to his room and flush explosives down the toilet.

My thoughts turned again to throwing the TV out of the window, but that wasn't as easy as it sounded. It was mounted on a swivel bracket secured to the wall, and would have needed a 13mm crosshead screwdriver and probably a set of Allen keys. Tools I didn't carry. In the end I rebelled by festooning the room with my laundry, and then ripping a picture of Constable's *Salisbury Cathedral from the Meadows* out of a magazine. He painted it after a storm. When the rain stopped, I went out to see if I could find the spot.

The meadows lay steaming in the warm, wet evening. The sky was swollen with clouds the colours of a bruise, similar to those in the picture, and there was the silver cathedral, looking, for all its delicate stonework, like a Saturn rocket set for blast-off.

Constable came to Salisbury a number of times and painted the cathedral and meadows from a series of viewpoints. In one picture he painted a sky so dark his commissioner asked him to alter it to something a little less foreboding. In another, he decided to look away from the cathedral and paint only the meadows; the Royal Academy Summer Exhibition reviewed his effort as 'a nasty green thing'.

In the painting I had in my pocket, though, he seems to have been on his game. The stormy sky is cracked open with a rainbow and the spire looks like a dark sword pointing proudly to the heavens. Painted in 1831, a year after his wife died, Constable wanted to evoke hope rising from his sorrow.

The meadows were soggy after the rain, and insects were starting to bite. But the sunset managed to infiltrate the gloom, and I knew then that this was the most beautiful part of Salisbury. The fields still possessed a sense of mystery that the rather aloof modern city seemed to have lost.

An hour later I was in a bar called Qudos, watching a middle-aged man in a sports jacket and tie prance about the stage in a graceless fashion while beating the shit out of a Spanish guitar. And yet he wasn't the strangest thing about the act.

Halfway through his song I heard another guitar join in, accompanied by a low wailing. This came from a part of the stage out of my view; all I could see was a long pair of legs in a skirt. But at the end when the woman stood up, it was clear that despite make-up and a long black wig, she wasn't a woman at all. This was the sort of thing that stuffy old Salisbury needed more of.

A German couple had come to sit at my table. He was glancing at my trousers. 'Trousers with zips in,' he said.

'That's right.'

'I had a pair once. Very useful. I used to go climbing in them. But then I had a disaster.'

'Oh dear.'

'I lost a leg.'

'That's appalling.'

'He lost a trouser leg,' said his partner. 'Not a ...'

'I know what he meant,' I said. I had probably looked overly shocked, but the truth was I lived in fear of losing one of my trouser legs. In fact I'd had a dream about it.

The woman had seen my ukulele. 'Are you playing?'

'Yes.'

Now she was looking at my trousers, as if to imply: how could I possibly get up on stage with zips in my knees? I was reminded I still hadn't done anything about my stage image, and after the day's hiking I was pretty muddy. Not that anyone else on stage seemed to have bothered. There was a lad up there now wearing a baseball cap and jeans that looked as though he'd done the decorating in them. His outfit was the least of his worries, though. He was singing with an accompanist on guitar, but the two of them quickly gave the impression they'd never met each other before.

The singer stopped the song and began again. He shook his head in despair a few times, and then, in a temper, ripped the jack lead out of the guitar. The accompanist didn't know what to do. He looked as though he might burst into tears. The singer had no sympathy. He pushed the poor guitarist off the stage and sang the rest of the song *a cappella*.

From there on in the evening became increasingly emotional. A guitarist played his instrument with such aggression that a string snapped. He stopped playing mid-song, said goodnight and left. The transgender singer had a solo spot and sang a sad song about life at home. 'Home, it makes me feel alone. Only myself to blame.' It came from the heart. Afterwards she announced she had CDs for sale and could give singing lessons if anyone was interested.

These were hard acts to follow. But I was still riding high from my success of the previous night, and when my turn came I threw myself into my performance. It didn't work. After an evening of the *avant garde* the audience couldn't see the funny side of rhythm and blues on a ukulele. I was too mainstream. I was only halfway through my first song and people were already looking at their phones.

Since no one was paying any attention, I stopped paying attention myself. I was up on the stage playing away, but I was also out in the audience listening to myself. Then I was on the beach at Littlehampton lying in the sun. Then back at home chopping wood. Then it was 1976 and I was on a Freddie Laker flight to New York. When I came back to my body I thought: I am really hungry.

As I walked back to my table, one of audience said, 'Can you play "When I'm Cleaning Windows"?'

I said, 'No I can't, but I'll tell you something – if you play that song backwards, you know what it says?'

'What?'

'George Formby is dead.'

After the show I went across the road to the supermarket and bought a tub of mixed bean salad and a bar of dark chocolate. When I got to the checkout, the cashier asked me if I wanted any help with my packing.

Evenings like the one at Qudos made me realize I should never try to second-guess an audience. Just because I'd had a couple of good performances, it didn't mean I knew what I was doing. There was no shortcut to success in this business. There was only experience. I had to pack the forgettable evenings in my bag with the memorable. And whenever I cringed at how far from rapturous my reception had been I tried to remind myself how quickly I would be forgotten. The local acts who died had to face their audience the next day in the post office or Starbucks, but not me. I was gone. Three songs and I was out of town.

Besides, the open mics were more than just a performance platform. They gave my days a shape. The journey between one venue and the next was as much a part of this adventure as the gig itself, particularly now that I had been going almost a week and come to the end of my pre-planned route. For the next five weeks I didn't know where I was going to be from one night to the next. I was just moving vaguely north towards Cape Wrath, calling in wherever the open mics took me.

I left Salisbury via Old Sarum, the original hilltop site of the city. Salisbury's first cathedral was founded here, until the population moved down to the valley and built the new model.

On this blustery day all the action was provided by school kids on a field trip, running round with pencils and paper. The girls read the information plaques and made notes about the Iron Age fort and the Roman, Saxon and Norman occupations, while the boys did Wayne Rooney overhead kick impressions with a plastic cup.

The River Avon flowed at the base of the hill and I followed it for the rest of the morning, singing to myself as I walked; songs I wanted to add to my set. 'It must be love, love, love,' I sang, and surprised a woman on a bicycle.

I walked in a dream through the Woodfords, then left the river and began to climb until the landscape grew more bleak. A cold wind stiffened my face as I followed a grassy avenue flanked by woodland, a strange green road, wide enough for a racetrack. There was a stillness as I climbed up to a ridge. And then there it was! Stonehenge, planted into the empty plain in the distance, turning light and dark as the clouds blew fast overhead.

Under the huge sky it appeared small and vulnerable. I'd been here many times before; experienced it as a child, as an adult, as a parent. But I had never approached it on foot like this. I could see crowds swarming around the huge stones, and rows of parked buses, and traffic buzzing past on the A303, but I didn't feel the need to go any closer and read more information plaques. I was happy enough to sit on the grass here, surrounded by burial mounds. The stark permanence of the site transcended everything.

I came down into the village of Amesbury, where there had been a murder earlier in the year. The local newspapers were still covering the case: a man had died of head injuries in a pub car park; a soldier from the nearby garrison town of Larkhill had been accused.

In so small a place such an event could feel personal, and yet with something as ancient and immutable as Stonehenge in the next field, I wondered if there was a temptation to view life more objectively. How many murders had been committed locally since Stonehenge was built, and how many more would there be before it finally crumbled?

But I was just passing through; the village had to deal with it. The place was so quiet I felt like an intruder on someone's grief as I waited at the bus stop. It began to rain and everyone pulled up their hoods, as if that was how they wanted to stay until the village got through this bad patch.

I took a bus to Devizes, for no other reason than I liked the name. There was another rally driver at the wheel, this time in control of a double decker. Overhanging branches snapped as we smacked into them; any pedestrian had to dive for cover. I don't think we stopped once. We went down so many back roads I got the impression the driver was taking a shortcut.

Devizes was cold and gloomy under the threatening cloud. On evenings like these, English country towns appear locked up and under curfew. I found a pub that had an open-mic sign in the window, but it was for later in the week. 'There's a place down by the canal,' said the landlord. I went and looked and found an impressive lock flight descending 32 stairs to the Vale of Avon, but no sign of a pub.

A bus came past with Melksham written on the front and I jumped on simply because I wondered if I would find another bus that night. But then Melksham was even less promising, and now it was pouring with rain and it seemed as though the only light on in town was in the pizza takeaway. I found a railway station, but the last train had gone, and when I asked where the buses stopped, no one was sure because the town centre had been dug up for road works.

I grew miserable as I traipsed around and felt another wave of 'What am I doing here?' anxiety. My successes were forgotten. If I had another disappointing night, I might start to capitulate.

Then I heard the faint sound of a piano. I picked up and traced it down a side street to a terraced house with an open window. Someone was practising. I could tell it was a child, and it suddenly made me feel painfully homesick, because for all the bad experiences I'd had practising music myself, I had at least managed to get results with my sons.

It's very hard for a child to learn an instrument. Why should they want to do something as difficult and dull as practice? Instant rewards are the only way they'll make progress. Star charts worked well with my boys to begin with, but as they grew older they grew wiser. They kept re-negotiating the exchange rate so that a row of three stars went from being worth a video from the Spar to a trip to Alton Towers.

I tried buying them a Red Hot Chili Peppers songbook to offer relief from Schumann or whoever it was their teacher was giving them, but I knew I had to be more creative. After much thought I decided on the single most important investment I would ever make in their musical education. I bought them a PlayStation.

It was beautifully simple. Half an hour on an instrument was rewarded with half an hour on the PlayStation. The results were amazing. One son learnt to play Debussy's 'First Arabesque' thanks entirely to Sonic the Hedgehog. The other son owes his mastering of Django Reinhardt's 'Minor Swing' at the age of 13 to Fifa 2002. When the PlayStation finally blew up I thought that would be it, but its demise coincided with their reaching that magic level where being able to play the music was reward enough.

Many times over those years I wondered whether I was living vicariously. Was I wanting my children to be good players simply because I never was? But then I thought: so what? They were doing so well, and by the time they came to understand what treasure they were uncovering, my role was over. I'll never forget the day my younger son came home with Beethoven's *Pathétique* and worked at the first couple of pages all night simply because he thought they sounded so damn good. My study at home was upstairs right above the piano and over the next couple of months I heard him strip the whole sonata down to basics, then slowly build it back up again until he could play it – and I could whistle it. The process taught us both what a true genius Beethoven was.

The young pianist in Melksham was struggling, but getting there, playing the same phrase over and over. Then someone called out and the playing stopped. The lid came down and the child was already on the PlayStation.

The rattle of a diesel engine made me turn to see a bus pulling up at the end of the street. I dashed towards it. The driver saw me coming and, bless him, didn't give himself the pleasure of driving off just before I got there. On the front it said Bath. I was so pleased, I gushed with bonhomie, 'Am I glad to see you? I thought I was stuck here. I'll have a ticket to Bath on your fine bus, please, my good man.' He was Polish and didn't understand a word.

I sat down and wiped the condensation off the window. I had had a low moment. And when you have one of those, things can only improve. I didn't know it, but I was about to be big in Bath.

chapter four

the bath and bristol show

It was still raining when I got into the city, but by now I didn't care. I stepped down from the bus into the busy centre and was so pleased to have escaped the clutches of rural Wiltshire and be somewhere full of bright lights that I felt like splashing in the puddles.

I was ready for action. I went into a bar called the Pig and Fiddle, which advertised an open mic. Again, it was the wrong night. 'There must be somewhere else?' I said to the barman. He called out across the bar. I was told to try the Curfew.

The Curfew was a tiny pub with nowhere to hide. A lad was already on the makeshift stage – simply a carpet in a corner – playing guitar with his eyes shut, presumably so he couldn't see the audience, which consisted of four people not paying him any attention. I was tempted to walk straight out, but then I thought: why judge a place just because it looks grim and the audience is sparse and uninterested, and there's only one microphone so the sound will be rubbish? I pulled out my ukulele and said firmly to the barman, 'Who's in charge of the open mic?'

'Doug.'

'Where's Doug?'

'Standing next to you.'

Doug had tight trousers and a firm handshake. He said, 'Ukulele! Great! Look everyone, a ukulele.'

One man gave an ironic cheer; his girlfriend screamed and said, 'What's a ukulele?'

'When do you want to play?' said Doug.

'Right now.'

I stepped up to the mic with purpose and was about to pitch myself into the first Chuck Berry song that came into my head when Doug said, 'I've got an instrument mic if you want.'

'A what?'

He produced a little bendy pick-up and attached it to the sound hole of the ukulele, then plugged it into his amp. This changed everything. I was free. I didn't have to stand hugging the microphone. I started to play and it was as if the ukulele had been given a turbo-charge.

From the start the small but perfectly formed crowd was with me. Four lads started slapping their table in rhythm. A group of young women tried to compete with them by clapping along. Soon the whole pub was swinging. Okay, the whole pub was the size of a cupboard, but it had 10 people squashed into it and I was happy with that. When the kazoo solo came they all cheered, and at the end of the song I got a roar that brought people in off the street thinking there was a stripper on. I had even managed to get a reaction from the hardest group of all to please, the drinkers at the bar.

I played three songs and they all got the same response. I looked at Doug to see when he wanted me to stop, but he just shrugged and signalled to keep going. The old rhythm and blues numbers were the most effective and so I happily rattled through the Elderly Brothers set. There was a 30-year age difference between me and my audience, but the music bridged the gap effortlessly, and when I played 'Route 66', two women at the bar left their stools and started jiving in front of me.

I laughed as I sang, and in the blink of an eye saw myself standing outside the pizza takeaway on Melksham High Street in what must have been my parallel life. The door onto the bus was a portal that had opened just at the right moment.

One of the dancers fell over. The crowd was getting out of hand. I would have played something slower but I didn't know anything slower. Then they knocked into the amp and it wobbled and would have fallen off its stand if Doug hadn't grabbed it. It was time to stop for health and safety reasons.

As I was packing away, a young thing came up to me and said, 'Have you got a CD?'

'Of course he hasn't got a CD,' said her embarrassed boyfriend and pulled her away.

Doug bought me a beer. He was an open-mic baron who ran three different evenings a week around the city. He had business cards and his phone kept ringing.

'On a midweek night a good open mic can bring in plenty of business,' he said. 'Landlords are gagging for them.'

There were once open-mic turf wars in Bath. 'One man who shall remain nameless thought he could run the whole network.' I got the impression it had ended messily. Now there was a free market and the scene was booming.

'The important thing is to keep your good acts happy,' said Doug. 'You don't want to go letting other promoters muscle in.' Then he moved closer and asked me to come and play at a session he ran in a pub called Ye Olde Farmhouse not far away. 'Tomorrow night,' he said. 'I guarantee you'll go down a treat.'

I said maybe. For some reason the idea of playing two nights in one town made me feel uncomfortable. One night I could get away with. Two, and people might wonder what they had seen in me the first night. But then he said quietly, 'If you come and play at the Farmhouse tomorrow …', and I really thought he was going to offer me money, 'you'll get a free bowl of curry.'

'Curry?'

'Curry.'

That swung it. I was being paid in curry and couldn't have been happier.

I had family to stay with just out of town. A big bed and a fridge to help myself from. When everyone had gone to school and work the following morning, I sat down at the computer with toast, and tried to plan a route for the next few days.

Finding places to play was easy enough, it was finding them on the right night and in the right direction that required organization. I didn't want to travel north one day and south the next, and I didn't want to sit around waiting for a couple of nights.

Bristol had plenty of places to play, so did Cheltenham. That was fine. I could spend the weekend travelling up through the Cotswolds. Then there was Oxford to the east, or South Wales to the west, or head straight north to Birmingham. How did a wandering minstrel cope before Facebook? Very nicely, according to the record. His route was determined by fairs, and, come the evening, he'd knock on the door of a manor house and ask to entertain the squire during dinner, earning himself a meal and a bed for the night. Try turning up at a manor house and singing for your supper these days and you won't get past the CCTV on the gate.

I walked back into Bath on the Kennet and Avon Canal towpath. This was near the western edge of the inland waterways network. Beyond here lay the tidal River Avon and the Bristol Channel, so for most boats Bath was a turning point.

I saw one narrowboat with Nantwich written on the side and the owner sitting on deck with his laptop. He'd come all the way from Cheshire, a whole summer's cruise. He seemed to be on his own and I wondered what he did for crew.

'Friends join me for a week at a time,' he said.

What better way to enjoy your retirement than cruising round the country spending short periods with all your friends. 'A week can be a bit long with some of them,' he demurred.

I asked him what the highlights of the trip had been. 'Best bit was coming through Oxford on the Thames. Worst bit was in Stoke where someone threw a tin of ravioli at me from a bridge.'

'Ouch.'

'Didn't hit me. Took a chunk out of the roof, though.'

'I didn't know you could get ravioli in tins.'

'Oh yes … It wasn't very nice.'

'You ate it?'

'Why not?'

Gulls gave Bath the sound of the coast, and with a wide stretch of the Avon flowing through the middle of the city there was the open space and sky of a port. The honey-coloured stone and the Georgian curves of the buildings were so well known they drew visitors from all over the planet. They wandered around in brightly coloured rain gear, not really sure what to do with themselves once they'd seen the Roman Baths.

Where tourists go, buskers will follow. A grizzly man in a wet overcoat played his guitar in the square in front of the Abbey. His voice bounced off the walls as he sang a Bob Dylan song, and then scolded a group of Spanish kids who were playing football around him, using him as a goal post.

I went into the nearby Pump Room, lured in by the sound of 'Somewhere Over The Rainbow' being played on the piano. The information boards assured me the Pump Room had been the 'centre of polite society in Bath for over two centuries'. Why, even Jane Austen had given an endorsement in *Northanger Abbey*: 'Every creature in Bath … was to be seen in the room at different periods of the fashionable hours.'

Times change. The young man at the piano in a dinner jacket played Chopin mixed with James Bond themes to an almost empty room. It was the tea-time sitting and a French family sat alone eating salads that crunched as they were munched. I wished my mother was still alive so I could have taken tea with her and ordered cakes on a cake stand, and a selection of sandwiches with the crusts cut off.

I settled for a glass of spa water, straight from the font that looked over the Roman Baths. A sign said *50p a glass* but the nice waitress gave me one for free. Another endorsement here, this time from that intrepid traveller Celia Fiennes, who journeyed the length of the country on horseback at a time when women didn't do that sort of thing. In 1687 she came through Bath, and in her book *Through England on a Side Saddle* she described trying the spa water: 'tastes like the water that boyles eggs, has such a smell, but the nearer the pumpe you drinke it the hotter and less offencive and more spiriteous'.

I sampled it like wine: stuck my nose in it and held it to the light, swirled it round my palate. It was warm and soupy, and tasted like someone had drunk it before.

'Tastes like bath water, if you ask me,' said an American.

'Honestly,' said his wife, 'he's made jokes like that all over England.'

'Why do they all play guitar?' a woman had said to me at one open mic. 'Why can't they play a trumpet or something different?' She had a point. For every violinist or keyboard player I'd seen, there had been 20 guitarists. And I'd yet to see a trumpet player.

But the guitar has become the instrument of choice for good reason. It's easy to get started; you can sing while you're playing – try doing that on a trumpet; it's one of the few instruments, along with the piano, on which you can play a rhythm and a melody at the same time; it looks sexy; and above all, it's portable.

The only problem with it is this: as soon as anyone learns to play the guitar they think they're a songwriter.

My heart sank whenever a performer got up and said something like, 'I'm just going to play a few songs I wrote when I was going through a particularly difficult time.' You could feel everyone in the room stiffen and prepare themselves for 15 minutes of torture during which the singer would give intimate details of his (they were usually men) desperate love life, which was either a cry for help before he went home and killed himself, or a cry for help before he went home and killed his girlfriend.

I always applauded them, of course. I had to, I knew what they were going through. I used to write songs like that myself, until I was advised to stop on mental health grounds. They were so miserable friends would wail when I played them and threaten to self-harm, then put on Leonard Cohen records to cheer themselves up.

It took a while, but eventually I realized it was a lot more fun to play other people's songs, and leave the writing to those who could do it. I just wished that once on this trip I'd hear a songwriter who wasn't awful. Maybe even good. There must have been one or two of them out there somewhere.

That night at Ye Olde Farmhouse it finally happened.

It was a similar sort of pub to the Curfew the previous evening: small and unimportant to anyone but the locals. It had been a jazz venue for many years, but now it was another in Doug's growing open-mic portfolio.

Doug wasn't actually there. He was probably off doing a deal with Richard Branson, and had sub-contracted this gig out to a friend. Things got off to a shaky start. Performers had to compete with the group of lads playing pool in the back of the pub and swearing at high volume. One performer sang John Lennon's 'Imagine' to a chorus of obscenities.

Eventually, the barman, using language twice as bad as the pool players, told them to shut up. They were suddenly very meek. 'We didn't mean to cause offence.' They even tried to pay attention to the open mic, and for their sins, had to listen to someone sing the song Tom Jones took to number one in the sixties: 'The Green, Green Grass of Home'. It was more penance than they deserved and the singer was lucky he didn't get an eight ball thrown at him.

When my turn came, I was given the sort of introduction I couldn't possibly live up to. 'You may have heard him last night at the Curfew where the whole place was jumping.

Bath has never seen or heard anything like it. Please give a big welcome to … what's his name?'

The audience crushed the stage expecting to see Rod Stewart walk in the door. Instead I got up, with my coat hanger round my neck and my little ukulele in my hand, and they looked at me with such a mixture of awe and disappointment I really wondered if I was capable of playing at all. But then I heard ukulele music coming from somewhere and when I looked down I saw it was me.

There was nothing to worry about. The instrument mic did the trick again and once more the crowd were behind me from the start, clapping out the time and singing the choruses to anything they knew. And the great thing about rhythm and blues is that anyone who can count to 12 can play along if they know three chords. I was allowed to do the first song by myself, but after that a harmonica player joined in, then someone produced a Cajon drum. Then I heard a flute! I couldn't work out where it was coming from, but then looked behind the bar and there was the barman playing blues flute, and next to him the landlord on tambourine. It only needed the foul-mouthed pool players to pick up a saxophone each and we'd really have been rocking.

I played four songs and stepped down with my reputation intact. The next act was a teenage girl with a guitar and she said, 'Just going to play a few songs of mine,' and I thought, time to see what's happened to my curry. But as I soon as she started to play I had to stop.

Unlike every other guitarist I'd seen in the past week she didn't try to beat the hell out of the thing. She had an easy jazz-slap style, and knew that it was just as much about what you didn't play as what you did. Then she started to sing. And that was when everyone stopped what they were doing and turned to listen.

People must have heard her before – she played the open-mic circuit – but it was as if she surprised them each time. I could say she sounded a bit like k.d. lang or someone else famous, but in truth she sounded like no one else. She had a voice and style all her own and songs to go with it. No one joined in with her, partly because they couldn't have kept up, mainly because they didn't want to break the spell.

Afterwards I made a point of telling her how much I'd enjoyed her songs. She was unassuming and a little coy, but she must have had some confidence to get up and play like that. I think I told her to keep going, to get all the experience she could, to keep writing, and who knew what might happen.

But everyone must have told her that. And maybe she wasn't even ambitious; maybe this was all she wanted: to play for fun, without any pressure, sing for the love of it. There was nothing wrong with that.

'Good luck,' I said to her, and she wished me the same, although our musical careers were at different points on the scale and heading in opposite directions.

I left shortly after that. As I walked down the hill I had two thoughts: 1) I had seen the real thing tonight, and 2) I never had any curry.

It was hard to leave Bath. I could have played in a different venue each evening for a fortnight, and the locals liked what I played so much I felt I could have done a turn at the Pump Room and had them jiving away.

It was all down to the instrument mic. It had to be. On both nights it had given me a richer sound. I convinced myself that if I bought one I would go down just as well anywhere. So the next day I caught the train to Bristol. I bought an acoustic pick-up and stuck it to my ukulele. Via a jack lead I could now connect myself to anyone's system. I was wired for sound.

Bristol had an even more lively music scene than Bath. I found an open mic on a boat of all places, an old Severn Trow, permanently moored to the harbourside and converted into a cosy bar called Under the Stars. It was perfect, and on a Friday night looked as though it would get busy. I was told to come back at eight when things got started.

Three hours to kill. I walked round town trying to find a hat. A performance hat. I'd decided that was what I needed to draw eyes away from the unironed, unbrushed rest of me; something I could slip on that would turn me into the Uke of Wallington. Didn't have to be a hat of course. Some blue suede shoes would have done it. Or a pair of sunglasses. An arrow through the head kit. I settled on a hat, a straw trilby from Poundland. It made me look jaunty.

I walked up to Clifton in the rain, to where the stately old lady of a suspension bridge spans the Avon Gorge. This was one of Brunel's greatest hits and under the leaden sky it looked like a perfectly organic structure, as if it had grown out of the hillside. Far below, the River Avon, which had appeared so handsome in Bath, was now a victim of the low tide, and flowed in a mere stream between the steep muddy banks. It looked a long way down no matter how much water was in there.

I wondered why there were police cars parked on the approaches, and then I saw signs for the Samaritans on the bridge supports with a phone number for help. The police weren't waiting to spot potential suicides, were they? Maybe Friday evening during rush hour was premium time. Suddenly, they were leaping out of their cars and running over the bridge towards me. I had my hood up for the drizzle and my hands deep in my pockets, and I thought: they think I'm going to jump.

I stopped and got ready to surrender. But they ran right past me to a woman who was hurrying across with a couple of Sainsbury's bags and couldn't hear their calls because of her headphones. They grabbed her and led her off. She didn't look like a potential suicide to me. She looked more like someone going home with her shopping. But they put her in a police car as reinforcements arrived. I asked the bridgekeeper in his little hut what was going on and he said, 'They don't tell me anything.'

I came down to the riverside, to the city's floating harbour, a locked piece of water with the tidal river diverted around it.

Brunel's SS *Great Britain* – another of his big hits – is the most famous resident here. When she was built in 1843 she was the biggest boat on the seas, and was the first iron-hulled steamer to cross the Atlantic. In her time she served as a passenger vessel first to America and then Australia, transporting prospectors to a number of gold rushes, and in 1861 the first England cricket team to tour Down Under. In retirement she went out to the Falklands, where she was used as a coal store and even a quarantine boat, until she was scuttled there in 1937.

Scuttling would mean the end for most ships, but the SS *Great Britain* was miraculously refloated and towed back to Bristol, through the huge locks, and into the same dry dock she was built in. She sits there now, fully restored, sitting on a glass plate so you can go below and sort of look up her skirt. A ship that lived happily ever after.

The harbour locks are used mostly by leisure craft now, the vast capacity wasted on the few small boats adventurous enough to take the drop down to Avonmouth and the Bristol Channel. The whole harbour looked rather redundant. No one working, no boats being loaded. A supermarket trolley lay in the mud below, wheels in the air, summing up the spirit of it all.

Dark clouds were moving in on the city and it looked like something biblical was about to happen. I hurried back up to the town. When I looked back at the bridge, it was lost in cloud.

The rain poured on the Friday night crowds that had packed into the city centre. Women in little black dresses ran from bar to bar; men toughed it out, standing smoking under awnings.

The bars were all busy, all that is except Under the Stars. When I went in only a few tables were occupied and no one was organizing the open mic. 'Don't know where he is,' said the barmaid. 'I should come back in about a half hour. He'll be here then. Be more lively.'

I was tired of wandering round. I went and got a macaroni salad from Tesco Express and sat on a bench. From a restaurant behind me a woman in a cocktail dress came out with a large cake. 'Here, do you want this?'

'What?'

'Go on, have it. They're just going to chuck it.'

Behind her I could see a function of some sort going on. Piles of food. Bottles of wine. I looked at the cake, a huge chocolate job covered in cream.

'That's very kind, but no thanks.'

'Why not?'

'It's too big.'

'It's free!'

'I'm on foot.'

'It's a black forest gateau, you idiot.'

I realized she was drunk and if I annoyed her she might throw the thing at me. 'I'm sure there's someone who needs a cake more than me.' I looked round, hoping to see someone who needed a chocolate cake.

'Just take it,' she said.

What was I going to do with a cake the size of car tyre? 'I've got to go.'

'I'll get you some chicken legs if you want,' she called after me.

When I went back to Under The Stars it was even less

busy. Just two couples. 'Apparently, he's on a holiday,' the barmaid said. 'The fellow who does the open mic. He's in Africa.'

Another guitarist had turned up by this time. He was fiddling with an amp on the stage. 'He's on holiday,' he said.

'I know. Africa.'

'We can still play. I'll do a bit, then you do a bit. It gets busy about 10.'

He plugged himself in and as he started to play, one of the two couples left.

Outside it had stopped raining and the city was swarming. But Under the Stars had more bar staff than customers. The guitarist went on playing regardless. I was reminded of the band on the *Titanic*.

At last a clatter on the gangway and six women walked in. They got drinks and sat down at a table and started to talk earnestly with their backs to the guitarist. He was just a nuisance to them. Then another couple arrived. She was in a party frock; he was carrying a guitar. He asked if he could play before me because he'd only just arrived from Colchester to see his girlfriend and they wanted to go for a Chinese.

'Sure.' I was happy to wait. The place would fill up soon, everyone said it would. With my shiny new pick-up stuck to my uke and my straw performance hat stuck on my head, I needed a packed house.

The man from Colchester got on stage and said he was just going to play a few songs he'd written for his girlfriend Debbie. Debbie sat at the bar and tried to hide in her handbag as the small audience looked round to view whether she was worth it.

Having heard one wonderful singer-songwriter the previous evening I didn't think I would hear another the following night, and I wasn't mistaken. His first song was an angst-ridden number that gave a detailed account of how hard it was to keep commuting from Colchester to Bristol, particularly while Network Rail carried out essential track maintenance outside Reading. His second song was similar but referred to those occasions when he made the journey by car and got caught in traffic on the M25. His third song was about his cat, and how hard it was to find cat-sitters every weekend.

By the time he'd finished, the table of earnest women had left. He packed up and said to me, 'All yours,' and went off with Debbie to have his Chinese.

I was left with an audience of two people, a couple who looked so stiff they were either on their first date or had just decided to separate. I put on my hat and marched to the microphone. I had taken it as a personal challenge to entertain these people, to make them sit up and take notice, so that in years to come, when they were living happily in the Cotswolds with their young family, they would look back and say, 'Thank goodness we went to Under the Stars that night and heard that ukulele player. He saved our marriage.'

Most of all I wanted them to stay until I was through. I didn't want to play to the bar staff.

I plugged in my new pick-up and it gave me a pile of loud and ugly feedback.

I looked at my audience with a grin. 'Huh!'

The man supped from his beer, getting near the bottom of the glass. The woman looked sadly out of the window at the light playing on the water. I suspected I didn't have time to worry about sound quality.

'Good evening.'

'Evening,' they both said politely.

'Right, well, with it being Friday and everything, I'm going to start with a Dave Edmunds song, "Here Comes The Weekend".'

'Don't know that one,' he said.

'You'll like it.'

It was like being in their living room. I hit the first chord. The windows rattled it was so loud. The couple moved back in their seats and she buttoned up her cardigan. The bar staff looked up at me and shook their heads.

I turned it down. Right down. It occurred to me to turn it right off. Having amplification when there were only two people in the bar was a bit unnecessary.

A group of lads came down the stairs. Took a look at what action was on offer, saw the lone ukulele player and went back out.

I was glad. I had warmed to this couple. They felt like family. I played the Dave Edmunds song at an acceptable volume and they applauded gently.

'Thank you. Thank you very much.'

'You're welcome,' he said.

'Next, I think a little song by Chuck Berry, an early recording, which could be classified as the first real rock 'n' roll single.'

'Right.'

'It's called "Maybellene".'

'Don't know that one either,' he said.

I played 'Maybellene'. They applauded in the same polite fashion. This time one of the bar staff applauded as well.

But now I wondered whether rhythm and blues was really suitable when there were only two people in the room. It was dancing music. Something more moody was required here, and I needed to entertain them with anecdotes. I decided to play a song I didn't know very well: 'The Devil And The Deep Blue Sea'.

'George Harrison recorded this song,' I said.

'The Beatles?' she said.

'No. This was post-Beatles when he was going through his ukulele period.'

'Oh.'

'I didn't know he had a ukulele period,' the man said.

'Oh George Harrison did a lot for the ukulele. The story goes he used to carry two of them around, one for himself and one for anyone else who used to play. He even hosted the George Formby Association annual jamboree at his grand house near ...'

They weren't listening any more. I was wittering.

I played 'The Devil And The Deep Blue Sea'. I forgot the words and messed up the chords in the middle eight. As I came to the end, the ribbon I had round my neck that supported the ukulele slipped its hook and the thing fell away. I missed the last chord entirely.

Their applause was wavering; I was losing them. I had

to do one more or I might never play again. I went back to R&B, a reliable standard, 'Riding On The L&N'. And I played it with all my body. I put my shoulders into it. I howled the tune. I gripped the kazoo tightly in my teeth. Halfway though the solo, I saw the man empty his beer, get up and put his jacket on. They weren't going to walk out mid-song?

No they weren't. He came walking towards me. I thought he was going to invade the stage, punch me maybe. Where was security? But he sort of walked right through me. Then disappeared into the door behind marked *Toilets*.

I got to the end of the song. Only one person applauded. The other one flushed the cistern.

Afterwards the barmaid offered me a beer. 'Sorry it's so quiet,' she said. 'It's normally packed on a Friday.'

'It could have been worse. Could have been no one in.'

Actually it couldn't have been worse. Had there been no one in, I wouldn't have played at all. I'd have had a Chinese myself, or I could have gone back to Bath.

As I left, I caught my reflection in a window. I still had the straw hat on. It didn't look jaunty; it looked stupid and I threw it in the nearest bin.

chapter five

never mind the hillocks – here are the cotswolds

Confession time. The first record I ever bought was Frank Ifield's 'I Remember You' in 1962. Try living with that for 50 years.

As a nine-year-old, I liked to think that I was personally responsible for the song going to number one in the hit parade. Just as I was for Frank's follow-ups, 'The Wayward Wind' and 'She Taught Me How To Yodel'. I was the only child in the neighbourhood with a Frank Ifield collection and I played it endlessly on our little portable record player, a Dansette, the turntable that powered the swinging sixties. You piled your 45s on a pole and one by one they crash-landed onto the deck like a dropped plate. A robotic arm swung across and Frank started yodelling.

The Dansette wasn't built for such abuse, and before long the arm went limp. This was a disaster in many ways, but mainly because my parents replaced it with a Dynatron, a radiogram with a polished wooden lid that we weren't allowed to open without permission. It was a piece of furniture more than a record player. The sixties ended for me the day I put a drink on top of it and left a ring.

Since then I've kept quiet about Frank Ifield. But now I'm coming out, because I've decided that one of his songs, 'Lovesick Blues', is actually very good.

It's a standard – others had already made it famous long before Frank sang it. Hank Williams, Patsy Cline, Jerry Lee Lewis and Little Richard had all recorded versions. But Frank's was different. It was upbeat and brassy, and in those days he had control of his yodelling. It was certainly his version I was thinking of when I decided the song was perfect material for the ukulele.

I needed to broaden my range. I needed songs for different moods as my experience in Bristol had taught me. 'Lovesick Blues' was catchy, but also quirky, an all-weather song that everyone knew, but everyone had forgotten. Above all, it was a break from non-stop rhythm and blues.

It would be a challenge to learn because it had more than three chords – although not that many more. I was sitting on a bench in the sunshine, at a viewpoint along the Cotswold Way, trying to work it out. 'I've got a feeling called the blueooos,' I sang, just as Frank used to, and there was a rustle in the undergrowth as the local wildlife evacuated the area.

I had picked up the trail in Old Sodbury earlier that morning. It was Saturday, no open mics, my night off. I had two days to get to the next gig in Cheltenham and I planned to spend the weekend walking through these hills.

I would stay the night in a simple Cotswold village, have a decent meal. I'd read somewhere that when Meatloaf went on a world tour, he insisted on a day off every week 'to recharge the batteries'. By that he meant a weekend of destruction and debauchery in Tokyo. I had my eye on a mid-price-range B&B in Stow-on-the-Wold.

It was a good day for hiking. The breeze had made the damp ground springy. I was walking without maps – that is to say I had forgotten to buy one, but the trail was well walked and waymarked and followed all the ridges.

And it could only be the Cotswolds. The panorama was so perfectly English it was as if someone had painted it. The valleys were full of woods and the path climbed and dipped over smooth-topped hills where the sheep were fat and cute, the sort you counted when you couldn't get to sleep. Even the sky was doing its bit for the picture: huge white clouds hurtled across the heavens, and, high above, a jet headed down the Bristol Channel towards the ocean.

This was a place of pilgrimage for walkers, of course. Laurie Lee had grown up near here in the 1920s, and recorded his childhood in *Cider with Rosie* before tramping to London and then Spain. Those lost days before cars and development sliced up the countryside are what the 21st-century hiker dreams of.

Like the fellow walking towards me now: backpack, ski pole, map in plastic wallet. He was in his sixties, probably just retired. Walking the entire Cotswold Way on his own for a fortnight's holiday. His wife didn't like walking and was waiting for him at the hotel with her feet up. This was something he had wanted to do for 20 years and kept putting it off, but he'd started to get knee trouble; it was this summer or never.

He strode with his head up, admiring the views over to the Severn Bridge and into Wales. I prepared myself for a chat about GPS systems ... but he walked straight past me with a brisk 'afternoon', as if he was late for an appointment. I felt snubbed. It was in the rambler's rule book, section B, subsection 6a, paragraph 8: two hikers passing each other on a National Trail shall stop and discuss equipment. I also wanted to have a look at his map.

I was walking through woods in the late afternoon when I heard the sound of opera music rising from the valley below. I wasn't hallucinating. It was Pavarotti, singing over a loud speaker. His voice tempted me off the trail and I came down into what I hoped would a classic Cotswold village, but turned out to be Dursley.

Pavarotti was singing at a garden fete, which had just stopped serving cream teas – the first in a series of disappointments that evening. Dursley was dominated by its shopping precinct and large supermarket, and in some respects had to be admired for the way it had utterly refused to exploit its Cotswold location. The first thing I tried to do was get a bus out. But the last one had gone at 5.30pm.

So I stood on the Stroud road and tried to hitchhike. This was a complete failure and quickly made me feel dejected. Why wouldn't anybody pick me up? I jumped about and put some effort into it, but no one would even slow down to have a look. I had travelled across whole continents like this once, but now these drivers made me feel shifty. A 58-year-old man with his thumb out? What was wrong with him? Where was his car?

I resigned myself to a night in Dursley. 'Only place in town is the Old Bell,' said a man creosoting his fence. 'They say it's haunted, but I wouldn't worry.'

I went straight back to hitchhiking again. Another half hour and still no luck. There was nothing else I could do but present myself at the Old Bell.

They had plenty of room; in fact, they looked surprised to have a guest. It was also very cheap. I was shown a room off the landing and left on my own. I lay on the bed. It was suddenly very quiet; uncomfortably quiet.

I couldn't help myself. I went online and discovered that the pub was once an assize court. Men were sentenced to death here, or sent off to penal colonies. The ghost was a chambermaid called Mabel whose lover had been dragged off to war and never returned. Mabel discovered she was pregnant and when she gave birth she killed the child and then hanged herself.

In room 6.

What room was I in?!! I jumped off the bed to go and look. But then stopped myself. What if I was in 6? What was I going to do? Start hitching again? Ask for a less haunted room? Best not to know. I was just up the stairs, probably room 1 or 2 – 6 would be on the next floor. Also there was nowhere to hang yourself in this room. No beam or anything. Although, you could string a rope from the window frame and …

I went and had a curry. Taking care not to look at the door on the way out.

The restaurant was empty. The waiters were lined up waiting for the Saturday night rush. When I told one of them where I was staying he said, 'Have you seen Mabel?'

'No. I just got there.'

'Don't look in the mirror.'

'What?'

'It's on YouTube, you know.'

My food came but I'd lost my appetite. A group of men arrived and sat at a big round table. They all wore well-pressed shirts and jeans and smelt of aftershave. They looked set for a good night out. 'On your own?' said one.

'Just passing through town.'

'On holiday?'

'That's right.'

'What? On your own?' said another.

'I'm walking the Cotswold Way.'

'Where's that?'

'Goes right through the village.'

'No?!'

'Yes.'

'Where's the Cotswold Way?' he asked one of his mates. 'This bloke's walking it.'

'What, on his own?'

'Yes,' I said.

'It's up by Painswick, innit?'

They wouldn't believe it went through Dursley.

'I once walked the Coast-to-Coast path,' said one of them.

'Was it good?' I asked.

'We divorced shortly afterwards.'

They all laughed. Maybe it was a divorcees' club. They came out in a group together first Saturday of the month. They had a few pints, then a curry.

'You coming to the club later?' said one of them.

'Where's the club?'

Back at the Old Bell, the earlier quiet had been replaced by the bass-line thump of dance music coming from the club downstairs, making the whole building vibrate. At least it would stop at 11 o'clock, I told myself.

I tried to watch TV, but the only electrical socket in the room that worked was behind the bedside table, which meant moving the set onto the bed and having it in my lap. But then the aerial cable wouldn't stretch. Throwing this TV out of the window was all it was good for.

So I practised the ukulele instead. I played 'Lovesick Blues' over and over. I read for a while and yawned, then brushed my teeth and tried not to look in the mirror. On the way in I'd forgotten not to look at the door, but I'd been relieved to see it was room 2. Still, I sensed this was going to be a long night.

So very long. At 11 o'clock the speaker volume from downstairs did change: it was ramped up to the top. The bed began to shake. Spiders appeared from under the skirting boards and made a run for it. Dust floated down from the lampshade as the hotel turned into Dursley's answer to Ibiza.

Midnight, one o'clock, two o'clock, the bass line kept thumping. I was in the middle of the Cotswolds, renowned for its charming limestone villages and peaceful rolling hills, and somehow I had managed to trap myself in haunted electro hell. If Mabel had walked into my room dressed like a chambermaid I would have grabbed her and complained about the noise.

At two o'clock, I considered going and asking them to turn it down it bit. 'There are some people upstairs who are walking the Cotswold Way, don't you know?' But I didn't think it would do any good. The bar was full of divorced men with eight pints and a curry inside them.

No wonder Mabel wandered about the place at night. How could she get any rest? I lost my fear of Mabel; I decided we were on the same side. I looked in the mirror hoping she'd wave back at me. I went on YouTube and saw a clip of a team of psychics at work in the Old Bell. One of them sat in the basement with a torch shining in his face, saying he was the spirit of someone called Joseph. They also reported the ghost of a highwayman on the landing by the cigarette machine.

At three o'clock someone called last orders. The music stopped and Mabel and I finally got to sleep. Shortly after that the church bells started.

I was travelling in such a meandering fashion that it felt as if I was barely moving north. But accents were changing daily and were like a gauge. Brighton cockney had bled into the Hampshire burr on the Isle of Wight. The clipped form of West Country in Wiltshire clashed with the broader version in Gloucestershire. Intonation altered from village to village. As I headed towards Cheltenham, I said good morning to a man sitting in his garden, not knowing he was dozing. He woke with a jump and said, 'I wasn't asleep!' And he definitely said it with a Birmingham uplift.

Another day walking the Cotswold Way, following the escarpment with more fine views over to Wales. Up on Cam Long Down I could see the entire Severn Plain and the Black Mountains far to the west, the Malvern Hills to the north. In the sky, gliders swooped with a whistle of the wind; below them microlights buzzed; below them came the hang-gliders, and below them kestrels hovered, flying for business rather than pleasure.

Ramblers' groups were out in force. I felt wrecked after my sleepless night and had to stand aside and let them stride past me, heads down, deep in conversation: 'Chris just didn't give me enough space. I wish I'd got out earlier'; 'I roasted them with cumin and coriander, then tossed them in a home-made harissa'; 'I got in the lift and there right in front of me was Frank Lampard!'

The ice cream man cameth. I bought a lolly on Frocester Hill and sat and watched the model aircraft enthusiasts at work, men with packed lunches and lapels weighed down with badges. I lay back and before I knew it, I was asleep.

Everyone had gone when I woke. The car park was empty. The ice cream man had lefteth. I hurried down to Stonehouse and caught a train to Cheltenham, covering more ground in half an hour than in the whole of the previous two days.

My brother-in-law's mother had offered to put me up. Sheelagh lived in sheltered housing down a leafy street. She cooked me Sunday dinner, and when I told her about my journey, she asked if I'd play something for her.

'Of course.'

'Wonderful. I'll just buzz my neighbour to come round.'

The neighbour came round. 'Have you got your hearing aid?' said Sheelagh.

'No.'

'Well, go back and get your hearing aid.'

The neighbour returned with another neighbour. They sat in a semi-circle, hearing aids turned up to 11, and I played them a Cole Porter song I knew. Their response was polite, but not overwhelming. So I played them some Buddy Holly and that did the trick. 'I'd have had a dance if it wasn't for my swollen ankles,' said Sheelagh.

You forget that this music is over 50 years old. When Buddy Holly wrote his hits, these 80-year-old women would have already heard Elvis, Carl Perkins and Little Richard. This was their music more than mine.

'How much do you get paid?' asked Sheelagh's neighbour.

I admitted I didn't get paid.

'Cliff Richard gets paid, so should you.'

I laughed at the idea of being given money for what I did. I would have refused it even it had ever been offered. This was a legacy from the Elderly Brothers. Our thinking was: if they pay you, they can sue you. If people insisted, we suggested they made a donation to the local village hall, which was where we practised and needed more money to restore it than the Sistine Chapel.

Later I walked into town through the Regency streets of Montpellier, on a balmy evening with diners sitting outside restaurants, and open-top cars cruising the wide avenues. Gustav Holst stood on his plinth in the Imperial Gardens, baton raised, conducting the ranks of begonias and petunias that sat up in rows around him.

Elsewhere in town Gerry and the Pacemakers and Herman's Hermits were advertising their shows. Imagine touring round the country at their age, playing music from the sixties. Some people never know when to give up.

The action that night was at a pub called the Cotswold Inn, a town centre venue you could hear streets away. The windows were open and a band belted it out. Drinkers had spilled onto the pavement and there was that good-natured summer's evening atmosphere that you get so rarely in Britain. Two women danced in the street, a man with a slice of pizza tried to join in. Everyone wore as little as possible; an intimate range of tattoos was on display.

When the band stopped I was told to speak to Dan. Dan said, 'Sure you can play. You can play right now.'

This, I was beginning to learn, was what happened if you turned up in good time. You got shoved on straight away because no one else had arrived yet. The regulars had booked a slot on Facebook or over the phone and they turned up like celebrities just before they were due on. The host had to keep them happy because they brought a crowd.

One man and a ukulele getting up on stage after a band has been hammering it out on electric guitars is always going to be a disappointment. 'Remember, size doesn't matter,' I said to the audience. But they'd already gone to get drinks.

I played some blues, perfect for a summer's night: 'Before You Accuse Me', 'It Hurts Me Too', 'Statesboro Blues'. This was ukulele music from the Severn Delta, rough and raw. I gave the old kazoo free rein, I stamped my foot in time. And I was turning them round at the bar – this old music is impossible to ignore. I saw the blues drifting out of the open windows, down the still streets, into living rooms; through the open-air restaurants all the way to the Imperial Gardens, where it pulled up sharply at the stern face of Gustav Holst who swatted it flat with a swing of his baton.

I got carried away and played those 'Lovesick Blues' when it was nowhere near ready. A big mistake. I went for the yodel and missed. I got the chords wrong. I played the chorus and sang the verse. When I looked up, no one would give me eye contact. When I finished, Dan came over with a fake smile and practically ripped the microphone off me.

A woman caught me as I walked off stage, 'Was that a Frank Ifield song?'

'Yeah.'

'First time for everything, eh?'

It didn't matter. I was just a warm-up act. I was supposed to be second rate to make the regulars look good. And one by one they were coming in now. A Paul Weller wannabee played some Jam songs. A woman sang a startling version of 'The Lightning Tree'. A local arrived with his dog, asked someone outside to hold on to it, got up on stage to sing 'Sitting On The Dock Of The Bay', then collected his dog and went home.

A singer in a black suit played his own material, strange mythical songs with Tolkienesque characters who all seemed to meet grisly ends. I always found it amazing on nights like this, that there were really this many people, in a place as *Little Britain*-like as Cheltenham, who wanted to stand up and show the world what they could do. None of them was ever going to get rich or famous. They all had day jobs. They came because they wanted to get away from playing in front of the mirror and climb up in front of an audience.

To non-players it must have seemed very odd. 'What is my accountant doing up there trying to play "Smoke On The Water"?' But I had tasted enough of it now to know that the nights of humiliation – when you forgot the words and dropped your instrument on your foot – were worth it for the nights when it went well and you skipped down the road afterwards with a shot of adrenalin running through your veins and a thrill that couldn't be bettered. Addictive was the word.

I spoke to the young man in the black suit with the songs from another world. 'Where do you get stories like that from?'

'Work mostly.'

'I mean the mythical characters like the many-headed king who got savaged by the … the …?'

'Griffins?'

'Griffins.'

'There are people like that in my office.'

There were some good players that night, although it had to be said the star turn, the act that no one could take their eyes off, was the girl in the red dress who stood behind a man with waist-length hair and spent the evening plaiting it for him in a variety of styles. This was hairdressing as performance art, and it didn't matter who was on stage, the audience was secretly watching her.

A band came on at the end and showed everyone how it was done. They brought their own audience, and they wore waistcoats and silky scarves, which is always the sign of a band with confidence. They played reggae, giving the evening a good upbeat ending. The lead singer even played a ukulele and I found myself doing what I promised I would never do: aspiring to get better, to practise more, maybe even have lessons when I got home, put a stop to this dilettante approach, take the ukulele more seriously ...

This lasted until I got back to my sheltered housing and discovered that I had my shirt buttons done up in the wrong holes. I had played Cheltenham looking like someone who had been let out of the home.

From Cheltenham I didn't really have a plan. I just went to the bus station and saw a bus about to leave for Oxford, where I knew there would be a place to play that night, so I got on it. It was liberating when decisions were taken out of my hands like that.

The bus driver was a woman. Nothing special about this, but you couldn't help notice the way she didn't drive round the countryside as if the police were chasing her. The reaction of other (male) bus drivers towards her was different as well. Instead of the usual raised finger or nod, she would get a big wave and a beaming smile. If we were in traffic, the window would be wound down and some greeting called. As we got into Oxford, and she dropped us near the Ashmolean Museum, the driver in the bus across the road blew her a kiss.

Oxford was a scrum. The tourists had moved in. All the colleges had broken up for the summer hols and the only students in town were from overseas. You could hear languages from around the world on Broad Street, where it was so busy there was no room left on the pavement. Parties of younger children on school trips were repeatedly being counted by their fraught teachers. 'Where's Gemma? We've lost Gemma.' They were terrified of the huge amount of paperwork that would be triggered if they arrived home one child short.

But then I found an oasis of calm, in St Michael's Church, where an enterprising vicar had decided music was the way to raise funds for his many appeals. Rob Terry and his jazz trio were giving a lunchtime concert. It was free, but the vicar wasn't stupid. He had deduced that whereas people were often reluctant to pay to come in, they would be too embarrassed not to pay when they went out.

He was also clever enough to encourage visitors to bring in their lunches and have a picnic in the church. The result was Rob Terry and his band played to the sound of sandwiches and fruit being consumed all around them. 'Whose is the egg and cress?' whispered one woman above the intricate harmonies as she passed a cling film-wrapped packet down the pew. It didn't matter; the audience were very appreciative. Not only were they getting something for free, they were also eating: the top two activities on any tourist's agenda.

The vicar also offered free tea or coffee – he was investing heavily here. But he was an old hand, and the audience were just off the plane. At the end of the show he stood blocking the exit with a verger on each side, and thrust East African Famine Appeal collection tins at the punters. They were putty.

Afterwards I went down to Christ Church Meadow, where I sat under a tree and had a practice. Before long two Spanish men sat down to listen. One said, 'What is that?'

'A ukulele.'

'Uku ...?'

'Lele.'

'How do you spell?'

He looked it up in his dictionary, but it wasn't in there.

With the day over and the tourists mostly gone, Oxford reclaimed some of its charm. The seven o'clock sun sent shadows down the narrow streets behind the colleges and made the stonework glow pink.

Before long I found myself in the Parks inspecting the cricket square, and dining off a Tesco chicken and avocado wrap. Just being in Oxford made me wish I'd worked harder for my A levels, and at least given myself a chance to come here. It felt so far removed from the real world it could have been Hogwarts, but there was an intoxicating air, the smell of knowledge, and the sense that three years spent studying here would change your life forever. I made a mental note to do things differently next time round.

At eight o'clock I turned up at Far From the Madding Crowd, an old-fashioned pub with a fashionable name in the middle of town. Once again I'd fallen for the line on the phone – 'You've got to get here early. It was packed last week. You won't get on the list' – and arrived there to find it was just me and the barman.

'It livens up later,' he said, as they all did. I sat and read the paper. A man in his forties came in and ordered a pint and then another in quick succession. He looked at my bag and saw my uke sticking out. 'You playing?'

'Yes. You?'

'Don't think so. Feel a bit ... tired.'

I recognized the nervous wreck that I had been 10 days previously, trying to think of reasons not to play.

'What do you play?' I asked.

'Bit of piano.'

'What sort of piano?'

'Nothing. Bit of jazz, blues.'

There was a piano against the wall. 'Probably out of tune,' he said.

Two lads arrived and set up the gear. 'Bit hot for an open mic,' said one.

I said to the piano player, 'There aren't many people. Looks like you might need to play.'

'I don't think I'd go down very well.'

A young guitarist arrived with a group of friends. They wore black and looked very serious. He asked to play first and his friends pulled chairs up closer to the stage.

He stepped up to the microphone. 'Good evening,' he said. 'It's nice to be here.' Then he gave us 15 minutes of social work put to music.

Another singer-songwriter wallowing in gloom, but these songs were rather different. They were well written, poetic and heartfelt. And so intense. Songs about broken homes and isolation. Abandonment and addiction. A bit of hopeless love thrown in as well. After each effort his friends applauded softly, and nodded knowingly. They were there for him.

By the time he finished we were all in such a state of despair the landlord should really have shut the pub. Nobody moved, the only noise was the till opening. I said to the piano player, 'Bit of lively piano music would go down a treat now.'

'Had too much to drink. Maybe next week.'

There was no one else, so I had to take my turn. I hadn't a clue what to play. Maybe 'Happy Birthday' – that would cheer them up. Or perhaps I should pick up the challenge and try to be even more miserable than the previous act ('and you thought your mate was depressed? Huh!') But then I thought: if this lot likes songs with memorable lyrics, then they're in luck, because I know any number of them by the best lyricist of them all, Chuck Berry.

I started out with 'Promised Land', a brilliant road map of a song, written while he was in prison, a black man's experience of travelling across the Southern States in the fifties: 'We had motor trouble it turned into a struggle, halfway 'cross Alabam, And that 'hound broke down and left us all stranded in downtown Birmingham.'

The effect was immediate. They sat up as if they'd just had their batteries replaced. Within one verse they were clapping along. The barman punched the air, probably in relief. The piano player was swaying to and fro. Even the miserable guitarist cracked a smile.

After that it was easy. I played nothing but Chuck Berry. 'Let It Rock', 'Rock And Roll Music', 'Maybellene'. I only stopped because my new instrument mic packed up and the soundman had to kneel down in front of me holding a microphone.

They gave me a sitting ovation, but Chuck Berry was the star, not me. His songs had rescued an evening that was drowning in sorrow. The young audience had come alive. An evening like this gives you faith in the redemptive power of music.

As I left, one of them said, 'Were they your songs?' He really hadn't heard them before, and I thought about saying yes, but would have found it hard to live with myself.

'Yes,' I said.

'Fabulous.'

'Thanks.'

Actually, it wasn't as hard as all that to live with myself, and it was probably worth it to know there's a guy in Oxford who thinks I wrote Chuck Berry's greatest hits, and could still be going round now telling his friends.

Coming to Oxford had been a diversion, taken on a whim. But I'm glad I went there. It left me certain of what I had thought was true for a long time, that Chuck Berry is the best writer of rock 'n' roll songs we've ever seen. His lyrics sound as though he made them up sitting in the back of a bus. But that's how songs should be. Their detail breathes life into every line and their spirit of hope and youthful restlessness make them all timeless.

All except for 'My Ding-a-Ling'.

I took the train out of Oxford along the Cotswold Line, a lonely route through stations with names like Ascott-under-Wychwood, Moreton-in-Marsh and Mickleton Halt, names so nostalgic it was easy to imagine you were on a steam train and soon they'd be serving brown Windsor soup in the dining car.

The line seems to have attracted more than its fair share of poets. John Betjeman was inspired by Pershore Station, and before him Edward Thomas wrote 'Adlestrop', the most gentle of poems to lost innocence, and yet chilling when one discovers it was published posthumously after Thomas was killed in a shell blast in World War I. He wrote it after his train made a brief unscheduled stop at Adlestrop Station one afternoon in June 1914.

The steam hissed. Someone cleared his throat.
No one left and no one came
On the bare platform. What I saw
Was Adlestrop – only the name...

He wouldn't even see that now. The station closed, like so many others, in the sixties. The one remaining bench from the platform – apparently with lines from the poem inscribed on a brass plaque – can be found in the village. In a bus shelter.

Many other stations along the line suffered the same fate over the years, and counting the number of passengers on the little train that morning you could see why. But at least the line itself survived and it carried me in its own time to the Malvern Hills. I got a bus to Hollybush, at the southern end of the range, and from there I could walk to Great Malvern.

As the bus dropped me off and motored away down the hill, it was suddenly very quiet, and I had my own little Adlestrop moment, defined as that silence and concentration between moments of change when all detail is exaggerated. Above me was a brooding sky, the same colour as the tarmac road. I could smell rain. A bee suckled into a foxglove. I swung my pack on my back and the only sound was my footsteps on the gravel track.

Walking the Malvern ridge was like being atop the back of a beast, a dinosaur of a ridgeway. I climbed up to British Camp – a Roman fortification – where the slopes of the ramparts were as smooth as a golf course and I could look over the Severn Plain from the opposite side now.

Despite the gradients, this was popular country for joggers. They all looked exhausted, but at least there were plenty of seats for them to collapse on. In fact, I don't remember ever seeing anywhere as well supplied with public benches as the Malvern Hills.

They were all sponsored and in memory of someone: 'To my mum Dora who liked to sit here', which made you ask what Dora sat on, because presumably the bench was only put there after she died. I sat down on one dedicated to Joan Bracknell by her husband and wondered if sponsoring a bench gave you preference, whether Mr Bracknell could come along and ask me to move because he wanted to sit there.

And where would it end? 'To my dear husband Pete who refused to ever come out walking on these hills with me, preferring to spend his weekends in B&Q where he dropped dead on Saturday June 12th.'

I saw only one bench in the whole of the Malvern Hills that wasn't dedicated to someone and that was because the view from it went straight into a patch of overgrown briars. Maybe you could sponsor it cut-price and dedicate it to 'My dear grandpa who liked looking at briars'.

The path rose and fell like a dipper for nine miles, over hilltops that had been bald for centuries due to grazing – the name Malvern originates from the celtic *Moel-bryn*, meaning bare hill. In recent years, as the livestock numbers have declined, bracken has begun to re-establish itself, to the point that conservationists have taken the decision to intervene and introduce extra sheep. It's hard not to feel sorry for bracken – waiting all that time to make a come back only to find itself up against the full weight of the Malvern Hills Conservators. But it seems we can pick and chose what habitat we have now. Something suitable for wild flowers and butterflies is up there with the favourites. Bracken is way down the list.

A steep path took me down into Great Malvern itself. Having got cathedral cities out of my system, I was now hooked on spa towns. Malvern was my third in five days.

The town clings to the hillside in Alpine fashion and, although it had attempted to look as though it was suffering from the recession as much as anywhere else, it couldn't hide the underlying superiority complex that every spa has, no matter how faded its grandeur. Every shop in Malvern seemed to sell antiques, even the deli. And then, of course, there's the bottled water, endorsed by royalty for centuries, good for the health and even better for the property market.

No doubt it was a cultured and hearty place to live. There was a bust of Elgar in the town square and he looked like a much more agreeable man than Holst. I found a room in a B&B, and the only other person staying there was a pharmaceutical salesman who said he liked coming to Malvern because it always made him feel like he was on holiday.

He drove 55,000 miles a year and was a Notts County supporter.

Open-mic night at the Great Malvern Hotel would, I imagined, be a sedate affair. No need to turn up early for this one. I could saunter in at 9.30 and show the locals how it was done. I ate upmarket that evening, from the salad bar at Waitrose, and sat on a bench near the library, a bench with no dedication, but which my sons might like to sponsor when I'm gone. 'To Dad who sat here once and enjoyed his salad.'

When I got to the gig it was packed, and from the amount of equipment stacked up on stage, it was an evening that took itself seriously. A hairy guitarist was singing in a growl, managing to make every song sound like a threat. The audience knew him well. They called out requests. 'Play that one about the anaesthetist!'

I found the host, Mike. 'Great name for an open-mic host,' I said, and he looked at me with pity, but was gracious enough not to spin me around and push me back out of the door I had just come in.

He looked at his list. 'It's very busy tonight. I've got the temperamentals in.'

I thought the Temperamentals were a band, but he was moaning about his regular performers, the audience favourites he had to keep happy, who got annoyed unless they were allowed to play at least five songs, twice as many as anyone else.

'Divas, eh?' I sympathized.

'Yeah. Divas.'

'I play short songs,' I said.

He said he'd try and squeeze me in later.

The hairy guitarist finished and returned proudly to his girlfriend. He patted her behind and stroked the tattoo of a bee in the small of her back.

Mike got behind the mic. He said, 'Thank you very much, Dave; big hand for Dave. Next up we have Mark on his ukulele.'

Well, that was quick. One of his temperamentals must have gone to the toilet and lost his slot. I wasn't really prepared. I hurried up on stage and fumbled with my equipment. When I got to my kazoo solo in the first song I realized I didn't have my coat hanger round my neck. I began to panic and ended the song after a minute. 'Sorry about that,' I said.

And there was my lesson for the night: never, ever apologize to the audience, because from that moment on you've lost them.

I played my emergency song, 'Roll Over Beethoven', but it did no good. A couple of guys stood nearby at the bar, trying to have a conversation. There were two ways they'd be able to hear each other. One was by moving to a quieter corner of the bar, the other was by staying where they were and shouting louder than the music. They went for the second option. As I sang I could pick up bits of their conversation about scaffolding. Then I looked up and there was the Notts County supporter looking straight at me. I smiled. He looked very uncomfortable. How was I going to explain this over breakfast?

As I finished the song, Mike was standing next to me, pulling the plug out of my uke. 'This doesn't work,' he said. Great. Not only had I played badly, the audience hadn't even heard me playing badly.

I was glad to be done. I could relax now. I looked for my salesman friend, but he must have been scared off. There was plenty to enjoy here, though. Mike played some good blues piano; in fact, he played for about 20 minutes. Maybe he was one of the temperamentals he had moaned about.

Then a teenager played keyboard and sang beautifully. She had a smile like Debbie Harry and great songs to match. I wanted to ask her afterwards if she'd written them herself, but she was surrounded by people telling her how wonderful she was.

A big man in a black shirt cornered her, introduced himself as Ray and asked if she'd come and play in his pub. 'Have you got a card?' he asked. And she produced one from her pocket with a flourish. Another man led her away. Either her manager or her dad.

I was left standing next to Ray. He looked at me for a moment. 'You played the ukulele, right?'

'That's right.'

'When I'm Cleaning Windows.'

I laughed as I was supposed to.

'Have you got a card?'

'Don't be ridiculous.'

The last act was a band with a violinist who stole the show and, to be honest, sounded a bit good for an open mic.

'She played at Glastonbury,' said a man with long grey hair by the door.

'Cheating really.'

He peered at me and said, 'Didn't I jam with you here once?'

'No.'

'You sure?'

'Positive.'

'I like jamming with a ukulele. Come tomorrow night and we'll jam.'

He was referring to another open mic nearby. The area was littered with open mics, he said: Malvern, Ledbury, Upton and in other villages around. 'There's sod all else to do round here.'

The next morning I sat at a computer in the library and discovered that this rich vein continued up through Shropshire and beyond. That would be my route north: up the Welsh Marches, along the Severn, via Hereford, Ludlow, Shrewsbury.

The A49. The Ukulele Highway.

You know, if there's one thing this country needs it's a good road song.

chapter six

shropshire: the hill remembered blues

The hi-viz jacket was all the rage in Hereford. The city centre was a splash of fluorescence as roadworkers, traffic wardens, police, even charity workers, worked the streets in brilliant yellow and orange. Maybe I should wear one in my act, I thought. As far I knew no performer wore a hi-viz jacket on stage. It could be the image I was looking for. An audience would not only take notice of me, they'd ask me where the fire exits were.

I was in Hereford to find a music shop, somewhere to repair my pick-up, which had lasted all of four days. Mike in Great Malvern had given me the name of a shop, but I needed directions.

'You know the Green Dragon?' said one helpful citizen.

'No.'

'You don't know the Green Dragon?'

'I don't come from round here.'

'Okay ... You know the Black and White House?'

'No. I don't know anywhere.'

'All right. Go to Marks and Spencer's.'

'Where's Marks and Spencer's?'

'Just round the corner from the Green Dragon.'

Eventually I found the place, a cluttered den of musical equipment with an assistant who didn't seem to like the idea of customers much at all, particularly ones with a backpack. I explained the problem with my pick-up, but to get it out I had to unpack my bag, and he stood there without a smile as underwear and toothpaste came tumbling out.

He tested it and it worked fine. 'Strange,' I said.

'Yeah, strange,' he said, making it sound as though he didn't find it strange at all, making it sound more like, 'Now stop wasting my time.'

I had an hour to wait for my bus. As I strolled back to the bus station, I passed one of the charity workers. She was rattling her tin but didn't seem to be getting much attention, so I cheekily suggested I could help her make more money. She looked wary. 'How?'

'I'll play my ukulele.' I didn't like the idea of busking for my own profit, but for charity, that would be fine.

She took a step back. 'It's quite all right, thank you.'

'I've got a ukulele in my bag.'

'No thank you.'

'I bet it'll work.'

'I'm going off for my lunch very soon.'

She turned away. I'd be telling her I'd been abducted by aliens next. My appearance can't have helped. After 10 days on the road, I had a leathery face and a beard that grew down my neck. At the bus station I asked a man where the stop was for Kington and he looked up at me as if I'd just insulted his wife. 'I'll tell you this,' he said. 'I've

115

lived in Hereford for 30 years and I've no idea where the bus stop for Kington is.'

If I'm honest, I don't think I hit it off with the good people of Hereford.

I was serious about a British road song. Here I was spending my morning travelling on a bus through the villages of Herefordshire, through places like Weobley and Eardisley where every other building was half-timbered in Tudor style, yet in the evening I'd be singing 'Route 66' and 'Promised Land', two great songs, but featuring place names like Oklahoma City and Albuquerque, Carolina and Arizona.

If only there were British equivalents. Billy Bragg tried it with 'A13 Trunk Road To The Sea', but that was just a pastiche of 'Route 66'. One excuse is that we don't have a travelling culture like the Americans. Our roads are too congested – any road song in Britain would involve sheer volume of traffic delays on the M5. And any journey we make can be done in a day. You can travel coast to coast in a matter of hours in Britain and see nothing but sheep, while in the States you can take a month and pass through deserts and mountains and Las Vegas.

The language doesn't help either. Motorway lacks the same spirit of escape that freeway conjures up; Little Chefs just don't have the romance of truck stops. We have a road sign that says *adverse camber* for heaven's sake. The opinion is that Brits should stick to writing the kind of travel songs they're good at. Like sea shanties.

This is an old debate, but I would never be in a better position to turn the story of a British road trip into a lyric. The Sargeants bus I was riding, with its bright red livery, ploughing the lonely route from Hereford to Kington, was as inspirational as any Greyhound.

I decided I would write my first song for 30 years, the definitive British Road Song. It would be called 'Four String Highway' and the first line would be, 'I stepped down into Kington Town. It was early closing that day.'

Well, it was. And when Kington closes for a half-day it really closes. You could walk down the middle of the high street without interruption. This was a nuisance because I needed to buy a sun hat. I'd left mine on a bus seat somewhere and would have to buy a new one if I was going to follow Offa's Dyke that afternoon. The sun was high and strong.

Then I discovered the charity shops were open, and there were a good number of those in Kington. I tried in Second Chance, but she had no hats. 'Try across the street at St Michael's Hospice,' she said. 'They have a men's department.'

'Oh what a pity,' said the woman in St Michael's. 'If you'd been here this morning I had an England cricket cap.'

'Shame.'

'Never mind. We've got just the thing.' And there on a hook was a faded blue sun hat. 'You must try it on,' she insisted.

She put it on me and pushed me in front of the mirror. I looked like one of the men on the bus in Worthing.

'Suits you,' she said. 'And look, it's even got a little zip pocket in the side. You can keep your loose change there.'

She was right, although I wasn't sure about carrying loose change on my head.

'Shall I put it in a bag or will you wear it now?'

'How much is it?'

'£2. You can have it for £1.50.'

'I'll wear it now.'

I spent the rest of the day hiking the Offa's Dyke trail, heading north through the Radnorshire Hills towards Clun. The sun blazed and the going was steep, but this was fabulous walking country, along a path that kept snugly to the folds in the hills, and then climbed steeply up to the ridge, occasionally even following the earthworks of the ancient dyke itself.

The dyke was built around 780, although it's uncertain whether it was a defence or simply a border. Whatever, it's a good name to have in song:

> *I stepped down into Kington town, it was early closing that day.*
> *I met a guy called Mike on Offa's Dyke, said it was the same in Hay …*

I did meet a guy on Offa's Dyke, although I'm not sure his name was Mike. He was with a friend – they were two old Welsh boys walking the path in the same direction as me, but much more slowly.

'Feet problems,' said Mike. 'Blisters.'

'We'll get the helicopter in,' joked his mate.

They were going to Clun as well. But they would never get there before nightfall at the rate they were going.

'We'll phone a taxi,' said Mike. 'We're not purists or nothing.'

Getting a taxi to pick them up from this hill would be harder than a helicopter, and probably no cheaper. 'We've got to get to the White Horse for eight,' they said.

The White Horse was where I was going. The White Horse was where there was an open mic. 'I'll see you there,' I said.

Found a bed by the river in the village of Clun
One of the quietest places under the sun.

The last line isn't mine. Local boy A E Housman wrote it in *A Shropshire Lad*, and I suppose it can be read as a put-down or a compliment, depending on your point of view. It's certainly a compliment as far as the tourist board is concerned, and they quote it as often as they can. But A E Housman never went to the White Horse Inn on the first Wednesday in the month.

It was anything but quiet: a busy local pub with good beer and grub, and everyone and their dog in there too. Literally – there were more dogs to be found at the bar than humans.

An ageing hippy called Eric was hosting the open mic. He played some good blues guitar with a gritty voice, and every 20 minutes he'd nip outside for a smoke to make it sound grittier. I shook his hand and he put my name down on his list, then I went and ordered a smoked mackerel for supper.

Two women sat opposite me. One said, 'I'm not fond of fish.'

'Oh, I love a bit of fish,' said her friend, and she leant towards me and said, 'Omega oils.'

She saw my ukulele and quizzed me.

'I'm just travelling round.'

'Don't go to Wales.'

'Why not?'

'They don't like us. When we go there they speak Welsh so we can't understand. They're very rude.'

'Wish I could speak Welsh,' said her friend.

'I wish I could speak Welsh as well, then I'd say something horrible back to them.'

I said, 'You want to learn to speak Welsh so you can say something horrible to Welsh people?'

'Welsh sounds good when you swear,' she said.

'That's a bit ironic,' said her friend.

'No, it's not ironic,' she said.

'What is it then?'

'I don't know, but it's not ironic. Spiteful, probably.'

My turn to play came. Despite the good-sized and friendly crowd there wasn't much interest. Too many people were eating. 'We're just background music really,' said Eric sadly.

But there were some good and interesting performers. A guitarist and a flautist, and then a sax player. After Malvern the previous evening, I was of the mind that the standard of playing was better in the country than in the city, and Clun reinforced this.

I went back to the women. One said, 'you played "You ain't nothin' but a hound dog".'

'That's right.'

'Elvis lives.'

'Don't listen to her,' said her friend.

A hand came down on my shoulder. It was Mike and his friend who I'd met on the hill. They'd just made it in time for last orders.

'You should have called that taxi,' I told them.

'We did.'

It was another quiet day in Clun – a painter up his ladder painting the gutters; a woman pushing her baby in a pram around the castle ruins; the butcher outside his shop spraying ant killer on the window sill – and I was standing by the river wondering whether to take a big risk. A bus had stopped right in front of me and I was inclined not to get on it.

'They don't come very often,' warned a woman who saw me deliberating. 'If you see one, you should catch it.'

'Where's it going?'

'Doesn't matter.'

The bus waited, and I watched. It was one of those dial-a-bus arrangements. Any local person could phone up and order a bus for the next day. When I asked the driver if I was allowed to travel, she had to check her book of rules. She put on her glasses. 'You're a visitor?'

'That's right.'

'Yes, I'm allowed to take you.'

'Where are you going?'

'Ludlow.'

That was the direction I was going too, but there was a path heading out of the village tempting me back up into the hills. I wanted to make it to Bridgnorth, but I had all day to get there.

'I think I'll walk,' I said.

The driver shook her head and the doors hissed shut.

The Shropshire Way, another long distance path, was going to lead me to Craven Arms. I set off waving a pair of blue boxer shorts as I walked, which might have looked strange had any passer-by not known I was simply trying to dry laundry. There were no other walkers, though. Just me and some buzzards and a stony white trail that wound through the woods and then sprang out into the open, presenting me with a ring of luxuriously pot-bellied hills.

'Blue Remembered Hills'. It's not possible to walk through this part of the country without reciting A E Housman's poem. It gets caught in your head in a loop. 'That is the land of lost content, I see it shining plain ...' It's like a song you can't get rid of, which is all right for a while, but, eventually, it's similar to hiccoughs; you need a shock to knock it out of your system.

Like a dog suddenly running straight at me.

I was in the middle of a wood and could see a house in the trees. A man in overalls was sitting on the front step drinking a cup of tea. 'Banker!' he called (or I think that's what he called). 'Banker! Banker!' But Banker kept coming for me, all mouth and muscle.

His tale was wagging, though, and he was fooling no one. He tore past with an unimpressive woof.

'I'm sorry,' said the owner.

Being in the woods and being multi-gabled the house had a fairy-tale look to it, as if it was made out of gingerbread. The front door was open and I could see bare wooden stairs and rotting window frames. 'Doing it up?' I said.

'Doing what up?'

'The house?'

He looked hurt. 'No.' And I realized I'd just insulted him, and his house.

'Of course you're not,' I said, back-tracking. 'It's lovely as it is.'

'It's a wreck.'

'No, it's …'

'You think I like living like this?'

'Nice garden.'

Now, the garden he did seem pleased with. The terracing and water features added to the fairy-tale appeal.

'The garden is where you've been spending your time.'

'It's not even my house,' he said.

'Right.'

I got going before he poisoned me with a rotten apple and threw me down the well.

'The happy highways where I went. And cannot come again.' I still had the A E Housmans, but that was to be expected on the top of Hopesay Common from where you could surely see the whole of Britain. The wispy cloud so high, the air so clear, and the hills rolling away to every horizon. It was just me up there and a lonely sheep, a half-sheared punk sheep, with the job of keeping the whole hill top free of bracken. No help from bused-in conservationist sheep here like on the Malvern Hills. This girl was on her own.

Coming off the common, I managed to get lost. Travelling without maps didn't look so smart now. I saw a woman out walking her dog and asked her where the path to Craven was. 'Haven't you got a guidebook?' she said sharply. 'Most people on the Shropshire Way have a guidebook.'

'I lost it.'

She told me to go down towards the farmhouse in the distance and then turn left.

'I don't want the road,' I said. 'I want the path.'

'That is the path.'

But it wasn't the path. It was the road. And now I had three miles of walking on tarmac with speeding trucks knocking me into the hedge. It was so dangerous that it wasn't until I got to Craven that I realized I didn't have the A E Housman blues going round my head any more.

Craven was a crossroads notable for a supermarket called Tuffins, which seemed the size of Heathrow's Terminal 4. You could buy anything you wanted in Tuffins, so I bought some Welsh cakes.

There was a railway station here and bus stops. It was an easy place to get out of, but nothing going in the direction of Bridgnorth. I would have to try and hitchhike again. I stood at the side of the road expecting a lengthy wait followed by an escape on the train, but before I'd finished one Welsh cake, a car stopped – two men with their satnav trained on Bridgnorth.

'Are you going to the steam fair?' one said.

'No, I'm not,' I replied, maybe too firmly.

They were out on a boys' weekend. Going to the Rally in the Valley, the valley being the Severn's, which offered them a double treat: not only a steam fair, but also a ride on the Severn Valley Railway. They could hardly contain themselves.

'Have you got somewhere to stay?' they said. 'Place will be packed.'

'For a steam rally?'

They laughed. How could someone be so ignorant of steam rallies? They marked me down as a loser who had no idea how to enjoy himself. What was I going to do for the weekend?

'I'm going to play my ukulele.'

The passenger turned round. The driver glanced at me in his mirror. Was I trying to be funny?

I explained, 'There's a ukulele club in Bridgnorth.'

But that was no explanation.

'I don't like the ukulele,' said the driver.

'Don't you?' I said.

'No.'

'Well, it's not for everyone.'

'You know what I don't like about it?'

'What?'

'The sound.'

'I don't like it either,' said his mate.

I began to hear duelling banjos and see rivers of white water. Of all the cars in all of Shropshire. This was why people didn't hitchhike any more.

'But then,' said the driver, 'I don't really like music.'

'What, all music?' said his mate.

'I like radio phone-ins.'

'That's not music.'

'I know that. But that's what I listen to instead of music.'

'Well, I know what to get you for Christmas then.'

'What?'

Yeah, I wanted to know what as well.

'Not music.'

It was a short journey, but seemed very long.

In the end I didn't get to play the ukulele that evening. I'd planned to spend it in the company of the Bridgnorth Ukulele Band, which met in a local pub, but I'd got the day wrong. It was a shame, although in some ways I was relieved. I squirmed when I thought of myself playing *against* proper ukulele players. I know 'against' is the wrong word, because undoubtedly they would have been very welcoming. But I still felt this whole trip was a balancing act. I was a hustler, riding into town, confusing the locals with my bizarre ukulele and kazoo combo just long enough to play three songs and sneak out the back door. If I put myself in a room with other ukulele players, I might be told I was doing it all wrong, that I was bringing the instrument into disrepute, and with the power bestowed upon them by the Ukulele Society of Great Britain, they would confiscate my uke on the spot.

As it was, Bridgnorth didn't need any more live music that night. I found a place to stay down by the river easily enough, then walked up the steps to the top of the town, where just about every pub had some sort of performer. If it didn't, then it was empty.

In the Kings Head an acoustic guitarist with a lot of equipment was at work in the courtyard. But he was so loud, everyone stood inside. Then it started to rain and so the guitarist moved all his kit inside, but he didn't turn the volume down, so everyone had to go outside and stand under the umbrellas.

I moved on to the Bear Inn, where a band called Planet Rock was blasting Led Zeppelin covers into every cubic inch of the bar. You can only pump so much noise into a room before the windows blow and light fixtures start to fall, and that's what Planet Rock was aiming for. A large lead guitarist with delicate hands was pinning the audience against the wall with his distortion. Presumably they were all steam engine fans. One 50-year-old dad was rocking away trying to teach his eight-year-old son how to have a good time. But the boy crawled under the table and played with his traction engine.

Finally in the Bell and Talbot a band called Squid was playing. At last some musicians who understood that an audience liked to have some oxygen left in the room. I said as much to the man next to me. He replied, 'I know what you mean. You can actually hear the music.'

'And you can hear the words.'
'Just shows it doesn't have to be that loud.'
'Exactly.'
'Exactly.'
We caught ourselves. A couple of grumps.

Bridgnorth was split between its high town up on the cliff, and low town down by the River Severn, the two connected by a funicular railway and some steep passages.

Whatever part of town you were in, it was the river that brought life. It flowed fast and deep beneath the sandstone cliff, a corridor of commerce for hundreds of years. Shropshire towns like Bridgnorth thrived once on this link with Bristol and the ocean. The old wool trade had depended on it.

I spent the next morning following the river upstream towards Shrewsbury, heading out of town across the golf course, the click and whoosh of little balls flying through the air making me flinch. The British Open was under way and there were probably more players than usual out on the fairway. I passed one man just as he chipped his ball very nicely towards the green. 'Good shot!' I said, as the ball bounced in line, but then spun sharply to the right and into a bunker. 'Whoops!' I added, and he would have happily bust his club over my head had there not been so many witnesses.

Across the river, the Rally in the Valley had fired up: lots of vintage engine noise and lots of steam – and lots of rain, too, unfortunately. 'Will all dog owners please pick up their dogs' mess?' came over the tannoy, so loud it could put you off your putt.

The Severn had made most impact a little further upstream, in industrial Coalbrookdale and Ironbridge. Throughout the 18th century, the river provided these sites with the all-important transport connection that eventually allowed the whole region to develop into such a powerhouse. Traces of industry were still visible in the undergrowth along the bank: brickwork from the blast furnaces, tileworks and river quays, redundant railway lines. All overgrown and museum-quiet now, but at one time operating day and night.

The jewel of the gorge is the Iron Bridge itself, and no more graceful a structure has ever spanned a river. It's so well cared for – brightly painted, well swept and free of motor traffic – it's hard to believe it was ever more than decorative. But these days Ironbridge earns its living from a different kind of industry, one that includes a teddy bear museum and bike hire, and everything must be spotless.

The Industrial Revolution may have brought prosperity to the region, but only to the chosen few, whereas everyone is in on the heritage industry. It supplies employment and has cleaned the place up, and, more importantly, no one has contracted an industrial disease. If museums do one thing, they let you know just how hard a working family's life was. There's a picture by Philip James de Loutherbourg, called *Coalbrookdale by Night*, and that's not a firework display in the background. It's the furnaces working 24/7. It looks like hell is just round the corner.

History is in your face in Ironbridge. Information boards are ubiquitous; there are so many signposts to attractions they stop meaning anything. The Pipeworks, the Museum of Iron, the Coalport Tar Tunnel. There was even a recreated Victorian town up at Blists Hill. Among all this, it was nice to stumble across a brass band festival, where bands from all over the region had gathered, taking it in turns to entertain the holiday crowd.

Brass band music just sounds so wonderfully optimistic, even the dirges have you whistling along. There was an encouraging range of ages playing as well. The old pros who knew it all had taken a back seat and given their solo spots to the teenagers, who stepped up and let rip on tunes that had all been written long before they were born. That didn't matter to them. They played with the kind of excitement you only get when you come across Duke Ellington for the first time and want to let everyone know.

Deckchairs came out. Ice creams and beer. I stood under the awning of the First Response team. A responder was standing there looking keen, but he was also a little disappointed. No one had fainted yet. No one had had chest pains. He caught my eye and that was all he needed.

'You interested in being a First Responder?'

'I dunno ...'

'I'll give you a demonstration; won't take long.' He had already got the dummy on the floor in the recovery position.

'ABC,' he said. 'You know what that is? I'll tell you. Airwaves, Breathing, Circulation.' He performed chest compressions on the dummy. 'Thirty of these, then blow in the mouth twice. Best to do it to a rhythm. I always sing "Nellie the Elephant". Not out loud of course.'

The Wellington (Telford) Brass Band played the theme from *Pirates of the Caribbean*, and I practised mouth-to-mouth resuscitation on a full-size dummy. Afterwards I caught a bus into Shrewsbury, just desperate for someone to collapse so I could save their life before I forgot how.

Shrewsbury was bracing itself for two musical events: me playing at the open mic at the Old Post Office, and Status Quo doing a gig in the Quarry, a park in the middle of town. The mayor was very excited. He was quoted in the local paper saying how he was sure entertainment of this quality would stimulate the growing night-time economy. He was probably counting on Status Quo delivering rather than me.

In the Quarry they were erecting fencing and a huge stage plus the kind of lighting system that makes you hope the tax payer isn't picking up the electricity bill. In the Old Post Office the floor show was more understated. Geoff the open-mic host had moved a couple of tables back and was banging his rubbish amp.

'Can't get this sound right,' he said, as he played his guitar with so much treble it made your teeth ache. He turned a few knobs on the mixer, but it did no good.

'Too much gain,' said a lad at the bar.

'Put a patch in,' said his mate.

Geoff had the shoulders and shaved head of a squaddie and he held his guitar like a weapon. I feared the sound quality was going to complete the battleground metaphor, and when he said he was just going to sing a few of his own songs, I was all set to put my hands over my ears or go and have a curry.

But what did he do? This proud man went and sang a set of honest and candid songs that actually made you feel differently about big guys with ear studs. He was a sensitive soul and deserved a better haircut. One song stood out, a lament on the way national flags are commandeered by the sort of people who make the worst ambassadors, like England football supporters. I complimented him on it afterwards.

'It's tongue-in-cheek, you know,' he said, defensively.

'Yeah, that comes across.'

'I get into trouble with it sometimes. People take it the wrong way. It's tongue-in-cheek. Really.'

Geoff let us know what he thought of Status Quo by announcing that anyone who played a song with more than three chords would get a prize. Well, that ruled me out. It also ruled out the duo on next who didn't play any chords at all. One gave a great beatbox show, the other sang like Shrewsbury's very own 50 Cent. They had their own fans in; they received two encores. If Status Quo got as a good a response down the road then they would have done all right.

I didn't have any fans in, which wasn't a bad thing, since this was probably my worst performance of the whole trip. The sound system, which should have been my friend, was working against me. It made the ukulele sound like a small animal being tortured and I sensed the audience were cringing. I was cringing myself. Then I saw a couple of people making jokes, clearly at my expense. I was only saved from complete disgrace by the act that followed me, which was so mind-blowingly bad that the audience probably soon forgot about me.

He was a guitarist who couldn't play, couldn't sing and forgot the words, and he crashed his way through 15 minutes, oblivious to the audience's reaction, which was largely one of shock. If Geoff had been a squaddie, he couldn't have witnessed any worse atrocity.

Afterwards the guitarist came and sat at the table next to me. 'How did that feel?' I said.

'Good. I had the audience right where I wanted them.' Then he gave me his card. It said 'Entertainer' on it.

I walked back through town and somehow got caught up with a concert crowd. But not Status Quo's. This lot were coming out of the Theatre Severn having seen Blake – the classical boy band I'd seen sound-checking back in Chichester. We were travelling through the country playing very different venues, but our experiences must have had some similarities. We were all performing, responding to nerves every night and to different audiences. The post-concert party was where the parallel ended. Theirs was Prosecco and canapés, mine a trolley dash round Tesco Express. That's show business.

I headed back to my B&B. Locals were out walking their pit bulls and every one of them said good evening to me, as if they wanted to prove that just because they had an attack dog it didn't mean they weren't pleasant and well mannered.

When I got back I read that at one time it was legal, indeed encouraged, in Shrewsbury to shoot with bow and arrow any Welshman caught within the city limits after curfew.

So that's why the locals with pit bulls said good evening. They were checking if I was Welsh.

The River Severn wrapped itself around Shrewsbury to the point that the town was very nearly an island. Any direction you walked you soon came to water.

A gale was whipping up the river the following morning, making life a struggle for geese and rowers, and littering it with leaves ripped from the avenues of lime trees in the Quarry. My plan had been to catch a bus out of town as far as the River Dee, then follow that into Chester. But the forecast was appalling, so I sat in a café and read an interview in a local newspaper with Francis Rossi, the Status Quo guitarist.

He was happy to tell the world he didn't do much these days except play his guitar and watch TV. He had tried to get himself a hobby in the past, to relax – he'd had a go at clay pigeon shooting, he said – but after a while, well, he just couldn't be bothered.

Of course, the man did have a hobby at one time, namely music. As a teenager it was probably all he thought about. It was what excited him. He loved it and it loved him back. But then his hobby became his job. As soon as that happened there was pressure involved, and accountants, and stress, and before he knew it, he had to do something as pointless as clay pigeon shooting to take his mind off it.

It was a shame, but I suspect it's the case throughout the music industry. Blake claimed they had hobbies. Skiing and eating Sainsbury's flapjacks were listed among them. This sounded a bit desperate and I suspected, like Francis Rossi, they didn't have hobbies at all.

And then you had the National Youth Chamber Orchestra.

I mention them because in a further attempt to put off walking in the rain, I went to hear their concert in Shrewsbury parish church that afternoon. They were clearly a group of talented young musicians, and you didn't get that good unless you'd been working at it since you could walk.

'Strong string playing,' said the man next to me, after one piece, and he applauded vigorously. I took his word for it. Then after another piece he said again, 'Yes, particularly strong string playing.' It was then I realized he had a child in the orchestra.

'She plays viola,' he said proudly.

'She must practise a lot.'

'Oh, a huge amount. Very dedicated.'

'No time for hobbies or anything.'

'Music is her hobby.'

I wanted to wave the Francis Rossi interview at him. This is how it happens. She had taken up the viola like Francis Rossi had taken up guitar: for fun, or because her pals at school were in the orchestra. Then she got good at it and very soon, by the sound of it, her hobby was going to become her career. Before she knew, it she'd be out there clay pigeon shooting.

I didn't often feel superior to musicians. Almost all the time I felt humbled by them. But in that church I realized I had something the orchestra, Francis Rossi and all four members of Blake didn't have. I had music as a hobby. I may have been rubbish at it. But that didn't matter. It was my hobby and I would never have to resort to shooting at anything to escape it.

I took the train to Chester, which in the wind and wet could easily have been Shrewsbury all over again. I only caught glimpses of it from beneath my anorak hood. There seemed to be just as many impressive black and white half-timbered buildings, and, of course, the River Dee was as predominant as the Severn.

Millions of pounds had been pumped into Chester to try and turn it into a 'must-see European destination'. In which case, what they really needed to do was float it downriver and tow it somewhere warmer. It was mid-July, but it felt like autumn. I set off to walk round the walls, and I got good views of the cathedral and Roman ruins, but when I came to the Grosvenor Museum I ducked inside, for shelter as much as anything.

Two centurions in full costume followed me round, just waiting, I knew, for me to make eye contact, so they could slip into character. This always makes me wince with embarrassment for the actors. I dodged them and went to watch a video that attempted to establish what Chester was like in the Triassic period. Muddy, basically. And I learnt that, like everywhere else in the border country, Chester had a historically poor relationship with the Welsh. As in Shrewsbury, a night-time curfew had once been imposed on them and, even in daylight, they weren't allowed to go to pubs. Nor were they allowed to meet in groups larger than three people, or 'carry weapons other than a small knife to cut up their dinner'. It made you wonder why the Welsh would want to come to Shrewsbury or Chester or indeed England in the first place.

I walked up the Hoole Road, which was a couple of miles of accommodation. Chester was once an embarkation point for Ireland and the New World; passengers would come up the Shropshire canal from the Midlands then take a packet boat down the Dee to Liverpool and wait for a crossing. I tried to picture country folk from outposts like Clun passing through here bound for California, but on this wet Sunday Chester was no inspiration. I sheltered in a bus stop and, browsing the internet, discovered if I went straight to Manchester Airport, allowing for the time difference, I could be playing at an open mic in Florida that night.

I found a room and sat and watched TV while cutting my toenails. Then I took out my uke and tried to work out the lead to 'Stairway To Heaven'.

I flossed my teeth.

There was no use procrastinating, though. Sooner or later I had to go out and find a place called Telford's Warehouse where I had been promised 'the best open mic in Chester'.

Eight o'clock and the low cloud had already made it dark. Cars whipped up the spray. *You're in the Historic Roman City of Chester*, shouted a poster, and I thought, so what? My hair was dripping and my shoes squelched. Cars had headlights on and drivers looked at me from behind their windscreen wipers, thinking: I'm glad I'm not him. The evening was going to be another disappointment, I could feel it. Who was going to come out on a night such as this?

I needed to ask directions, but there wasn't another soul about. The lights of a Tesco Metro beckoned and the warm doughy welcome of the sandwich bar invited me to curl up next to it. The checkout assistant said he'd never heard of Telford's Warehouse.

Eventually I saw a cyclist and practically wrestled him to the ground: where's Telford's Warehouse or else? He pointed towards the canal.

I walked under bypasses and railway arches, until I saw a grey brick building standing over the canal basin and looking like a workhouse.

Down steps, through an alley, until I found a door. I pushed it slowly open ... and it was like walking off the street into some speakeasy in 1930s Chicago.

The place was packed, and spread over three floors for dining, drinking and cabaret. A huge picture window looked out over the canal basin where rain lashed the water, but here in the warm a long bar served a wide range of ales, and down some steps into a cave-like space was a performance area with tables and low lights, and a stage where a woman sat at a keyboard wearing an evening dress, squealing.

Her name was Kai Lei and, to be fair, the squealing was part of an impressive vocal workout, which the audience loved. And what an audience: bright, witty and keen to have a good time. I found Kai Lei as she came off and asked to be put on her list. She took one look at the soggy specimen clutching a ukulele in front of her and must have thought 'What the hell?' and said, 'Sure.'

It turned out to be a variety show. A string quartet played; a guy with an accordion sang in French; a jazz pianist played a short set. At 10 o'clock Kai Lei took my arm and said, 'I'll show you where the Green Room is.'

Green Room! Well, okay it was just a storeroom with a freezer in it, but it led onto the stage from behind, and it was as near to the real thing as I had come on this trip. My call came and I stepped out into the lights and heard someone say, 'He's got a ukulele!' and I knew everything was going to be all right.

Outside, the mist wreathed Thomas Telford's old building, but inside we had built up our own fug. I played 'Rock And Roll Music' and had them clapping along. They sang with me on 'Maybellene'. Then, when I looked up, I realized the whole show was up on screens all around the pub. I could see myself playing the ukulele, and I looked as butch as I always thought I did.

Basically, it was like being on the Pyramid Stage at Glastonbury, and the applause at the end made me stand there, milking it. Would this be the night I heard that word I longed to hear – 'Encore!'

Kai Lei grabbed me and pulled me off with a look that

said, 'Don't get carried away sonny. There's a magician on next who can saw his own leg off.'

It was still raining as I left, but I didn't feel it. I was walking above the clouds. Now Chester seemed like a delightful place and I couldn't understand why anyone would want to go to Florida. It was beautiful and historic, the rain gave it atmosphere. It was truly an Unmissable European Destination.

I was experiencing the kind of thrill that made me stop trying to look for the real reason I was making this trip. This was what it was about: this glowing high, the kind you can only get from being on stage and playing well and the crowd laughing at all your jokes and cheering you on. Had there been another open mic in Chester that night I would have gone straight there.

Instead I went back to the Tesco Metro and treated myself to a packet of sushi. 'What's that in your bag?' said the assistant.

'My ukulele,' I said proudly, and if he'd asked me to I would have happily got it out and played him something right there.

I stepped down into Kington town, it was early closing day.
Met a guy called Mike on Offa's Dyke, said it was the same in Hay.
The Shropshire Way was like walking through Heaven,
Shrewsbury made me want to jump in the Severn,
But in Chester I took my uke out and blew them away.

I'm on a four-string highway
I'm on a four-string highway
I'm on a four-string highway.

Maybe it's not possible to write a decent road song about Britain after all.

chapter seven

no sleep 'til llandudno

I had heard such unpleasant things about Wales as I came up the Marches, I felt I had to go and play there and see for myself. Wales is the Land of Song after all. Surely, a man and his ukulele could expect a welcome in the valleys.

There was an attractive train line along the north coast that stopped off at all sorts of places I wanted to go to, but couldn't pronounce. There were obvious ones like Ffynnongroyw, but even somewhere like Conwy was a mystery. Was it pronounced Conway? Or Conwee, or Conwhy, or something altogether different like Newport? The town website doesn't tell you; no information site does, and I'd have felt rude asking a local how to pronounce his town's name. There was nothing else for it. I would have to get to Conwy and spend the whole day there without saying it.

Conwy's castle is so intact it is hard to believe it wasn't built in the post-war housing boom. It rises over the town like a guardian angel, with fortified walls for wings, and is impressive for the way it still dominates the modern urban architecture, rather than the other way round.

It looks like a proper castle with a high curtain wall and its turrets and barbican complete, plus characters from the 13th century still wandering around. Or maybe they were local people dressed up in costume. That must have been it. Only people who have accepted money to dress up as crusaders or serving wenches and pretend to be living in the time of Edward I, can look that miserable. One of them was following me around to the point where I turned and said, 'Can I help you?'

'Is this yours?'

And he held up the mitten from the top of my ukulele.

'Er, yes. Thank you. Thank you very much.'

He stood there, desperate for me to ask him a question.

'I was wondering ...'

'Yes?'

'This castle ...'

'Yes?'

'Er ... the walls ...'

'The walls ...?'

'Yes. The walls. How ... thick are they?'

'Up to 4.6 metres.'

'Really? 4.6 metres? Well! Well, thank you very much.'

'Is that all?'

'Yes, thank you.'

'Enjoy your visit to Conwy.'

So that was how you pronounced it.

There were fine bridges in Conwy too, three of them in a row over the harbour river: a beautiful suspension bridge built by Thomas Telford, a tubular railway bridge built by Robert Stephenson, and a modern road bridge built by someone nowhere near historic enough to get a mention, but which was just as important because it provided a good vantage point to view the other bridges.

I took a walk round the medieval walls. They were interesting because they gave a view of a town you didn't normally see – looking down on backyards and washing lines – and also because they had a practical use; local people used them as a thoroughfare as they went about their business: a man in overalls with a ladder passed me; a woman with a briefcase, speaking on her phone.

I ended up on the harbour front, where one house was getting much more attention than any of the others. *The Smallest House in Britain*, read the sign outside. It was little bigger than a doll's house, painted bright red, and almost built into the town wall. You could go in for £1, but a woman in national costume was on guard outside. She already had her eyes on me. I didn't dare go any nearer.

From Conwy it was a short ride to Bangor on the Menai Straits where there might or might not have been an open mic that evening in a Greek restaurant. The waiter I had spoken to on the phone didn't seem sure. 'Is like a talent show, is very funny.'

'If I come, can I play my ukulele?'

'Last week we had a belly dancer.'

'How about a ukulele?'

'And a juggler. I think is a juggler.'

'Ukulele.'

'I laugh so much.'

This was the first coastline I'd reached since Brighton, and it made me aware of how far I had already come. It was hard to get too carried away, though. A quick look at the map in the railway station showed me just how much further I had to go. It was still a good way to Newcastle and then Scotland looked enormous.

'Is that Snowdon?' I asked a teenager pushing a pram.

'Where?' She gazed up at the range of mountains behind the town as if she'd never looked that way before.

'Up there, the big one.'

She shrugged. 'I don't know. I'm not very good at mountains. My dad will know.'

All I knew about Bangor was that it was the place The Beatles came to in 1967 to spend a weekend in retreat with the Maharishi, and where they received the news that Brian Epstein had died. Normally a town with a Beatles connection is elevated to tourist royalty, but Bangor seemed to have missed out. It was a university town, but with the students on holiday it looked closed down. The only hint of excitement was down in the park along the front where there was a circus. A little big top had been erected. The tide was out and the seaweed had created a stinky beach. Not that the over-excited kids waiting in a line at the ticket booth were bothered; this was the most thrilling day of the year. Behind the tent the master of ceremonies had a smoke and tucked his shirt into his trousers.

The economic slump seemed to have hit Bangor more than anywhere else I'd passed through. As well as the many charity shops on the high street, some premises were simply boarded up. There was a huge new development around the university main building, but this just underlined the split between the town's camps. The university took care of itself. The rest of Bangor looked left behind.

The Greek restaurant in the upper town had done its best to liven the spirits. Walls had been whitewashed; some Greek signs hung up; a courtyard with trees had been incorporated into the design, and the whole restaurant was strung with fairy lights to re-create a little corner of the Cyclades on the Welsh coast.

There was something missing, though. People eating, that was it! This would normally be a bad sign for a restaurant, but instead of diners there were a number of musicians present, and with rather more exotic instruments than I was used to – both Greek and Celtic. One man had a bouzouki, another a bodhrán drum. I said hello, and they responded in Welsh, and I felt that awkwardness you feel in another country when you have to admit that you don't speak the language.

'Sorry I don't speak Welsh,' I said. It was no trouble. They simply continued the conversation in English.

They introduced themselves, shook hands – the first time other performers had behaved like this to me. 'We had a belly dancer last week,' said one.

'Coming again this week,' said another, excitedly.

Two lads called Dave and Don arrived. They were the self-styled Clwb Cabaret and hosts for the evening. They spread red and black cloths on the tables, and put candles out and even flowers in little vases. The nightclub setting was complete with about 30 people in the audience. Perfect.

'Let the evening begin,' said Dave like a compère from burlesque Berlin, and all the musicians in the room, apart from me, got onto the stage. They were all members of one band and they sang songs in Welsh and then in English, which, with all the Greek signs around, meant you had to concentrate to remember just where you were.

It was a good lively start. The audience wanted to sing and they joined in with any song whether they knew the language or not. The only problem was that when the band had finished I was the only performer left.

'Can you play for half an hour?' asked Dave.

'I've never played for half an hour.'

'Long as you can, then.'

'I thought there was a belly dancer.'

'She's not here yet.'

Half of me wanted to say no. The other half wanted to say no as well. But a tiny piece that mathematically wasn't really part of me said I should grab a chance like this. Scotland may have still been a long way off, but when I did finally get to Cape Wrath it would be good to know a longer set was something I had in me.

I got up to the microphone, a little wary. These were Welsh people. They might not like an Englishman singing to them. They may have had relatives shot with a bow and arrow in Shrewsbury. The best I could do was start with a Dave Edmunds song. He was Welsh.

After that I just played everything I knew. Then I played things I wasn't sure if I knew or not; and finally things I knew I didn't know. It didn't seem to matter. The audience wanted to join in with everything. I lost them only once when I decided to play 'Tiger Feet', the Mud hit from the seventies. I'd only learnt it because it seemed like the kind of song you should never play on the ukulele.

The whole room agreed with me and decided it was time to go for a drink.

'I'd better end there,' I said to Dave.

'Maybe you better had.'

The audience quickly reconvened and, encouraged by Dave, we spent the rest of the evening writing a communal song, which he then performed. It was truly dreadful. But I felt I'd made friends that night. I swapped email addresses with a couple from Caernarfon. Like everyone else they had come in the hope of seeing a belly dancer and got me instead, but they didn't let their disappointment show.

Evenings were busy, but the days were mine. No matter where I was going, I always had all day to get there.

I was heading back along the coast to Llandudno where, I'd been informed, there was a good session in the Cross Keys each week. 'The cream of Llandudno play there,' I was told.

Llandudno lay at the foot of the Great Orme, a lump of headland that stretched out into the sea like a giant paw. I followed the coast path round with views back to Conwy Castle and Snowdonia. A road had been hewn out of the rock in Victorian times to offer charabanc trips. It was still open to traffic, but all was quiet that morning, just the birdlife and the wind.

I sat outside a café on the tip of the headland. A kestrel hovered over a hedgerow and a woman watched it closely with binoculars. It hovered and hovered, and then hovered some more. This was all very well, but we're used to wildlife films on TV where there is a lot more action than just hovering. The woman kept adjusting her binoculars. I didn't dare look away in case I missed something dramatic. The bird hovered a little lower and then lower, and then finally dropped into the grass. This was more like it, but where was the close-up?

'What can you see?' I asked.

'Nothing yet,' she said briskly.

The bird rose up with something black and wriggling in its beak.

'What is it?'

'Vole.'

'Hope it tastes better than it looks,' I said. She glanced at me, sadly, then trained her binoculars out to sea.

I climbed up the hill and came across the church of St Tudno and its graveyard in a spectacular setting. If it's true and you really do have to die, then there can't be many more scenic places to lie for eternity. Church services were held outside in the summer, and surrounded by the sky and water you certainly felt nearer to heaven here.

Nearer than you ever would at the top of the headland anyway, where there was a complex with a cable car and tramway to ferry visitors up and down from the town. There was even a dry-ski slope. It was strange to see all these very human facilities in the middle of what was otherwise a wild piece of coast. Perhaps strangest of all was the pub right on the summit, which had been turned into a shrine to the boxer Randolph Turpin.

I'd never heard of the man, but the story of how he beat Sugar Ray Robinson to win the world title in 1951, only to lose it six months later and begin a period of slow decline, is a desperately sad one. Turpin had owned this pub at one time, an investment made with his winnings during the good years. Llandudno urban council bought him out in 1961 when the taxman came after him, but he was soon bankrupt. He was never able to cope with life outside the ring and committed suicide in 1966.

There was a Christian road block along the seafront in Llandudno. A group of teenagers was standing in a line handing out hymn sheets. They were in town for the week, they said, 'Just playing with the children on the beach, spreading the word, singing some songs.'

In between hymns the group leader would interview members of his team, thrusting a microphone at them. 'So what's it like being a Christian?' he asked one.

'It's fun,' said the girl.

'Not boring?'

'Not boring at all.'

'Tell the people why it's not boring.'

And she giggled and said, 'Because I know when I die I'll go to heaven.'

One of her colleagues was standing by me. Maybe I looked unconvinced, because she handed me a hymn sheet and said, 'You seem troubled.'

I said, 'Your friend sounds very certain.'

She smiled. 'What's wrong with being certain?'

'Well, it seems to me it might be better to learn to deal with uncertainty.'

'Are you certain of that?'

She was looking at me with unblinking eyes, and I knew it would be futile to enter into a discussion with her, right here on the prom. They had all the answers; they had all been through customer training. Also I wouldn't have got away before nightfall. I tried to give her back the hymn sheet, but she insisted I keep it. 'It's for you.'

'It's a waste.'

'You never know when you might need it.'

Summer was back. Daytrippers strolled along the promenade in front of the curve of grand hotels. The wide sands were a playground. The wind farm out to sea made the ocean look full of sails.

Dog walkers were out in numbers, plastic bags in hand, although it was the gulls that really needed someone to clear up after them in Llandudno. They strutted along the seafront like gangsters, looking for trouble, crapping with impunity. The dogs knew who was in charge and kept well away. The little boy running at the birds and making them take off was braver, but you knew they were just playing with him. If he annoyed them too much, three of them would gang together, pick him up and drop him out in the bay. Teach the pesky kid a lesson.

Then on the pier I actually saw a gull mug someone. A man was sitting on a bench with his family, eating an ice cream, when the bird flew in from behind and, with one swoop, grabbed the whole cone out of his hand.

The family was left in shock, not really believing what they'd just witnessed. I watched the gull wheel away. It seemed to have swallowed the ice cream whole – to hell with the headache. When calm was restored and the dad had got another ice cream, you could only admire the bird for its cheek.

I said to the ice cream salesman, 'Did you see that?'

'Happens all the time. One guy lost his pasty yesterday. I always tell 'em, eat your ice cream with your back to the wall.'

Llandudno was only 20 miles from Bangor, but there were as many English accents – Manchester and Liverpool – as there were Welsh. The resort was purpose-built in the mid-19th century with wide streets, pier and lido, and many theatres and concerts halls, which all boasted seaside spectaculars. Coming Soon, The Osmonds!

It appeared to be all for the visitor. However, as the sun set behind the town, and the bus loads of trippers left the huge coach park empty, the cream of Llandudno came out and headed to the Cross Keys.

I got there in good time, and for once there was already a crowd. I had thought there would be another mixture of instruments, harps and pipes, like the previous evening, but there didn't seem to be anything except electric guitars and stacks of amplification. The first act was a tough-looking band who took ages setting up. I counted four guitarists.

'What sound of music do they play?' I asked a lad at the bar.

'Sort of funk … grunge … metal,' he said.

After a long time they were ready. The first chord was so loud it would have annoyed the residents up in St Tudno's graveyard. They ploughed through two verses of

'Johnny B Goode', which sounded appalling and climaxed with a scream of feedback. Then they left the building and never came back.

Well, I suppose if you're the cream you can afford to be moody. But the next act was no improvement. After the overkill of four guitars, now we had a minimalist setup of bass player and someone sitting at a desk with his laptop, seeming to do all the work. At one point the bass player stopped and took a swig from his beer but the bass line kept on coming from somewhere.

Despite the pared-down line-up, the volume was up to max again, and now I noticed the pub was filling with goths. When the next act got up, they too were a grunge-funk-garage-punk band and by now I was beginning to wonder if the cream of Llandudno were simply a bunch of heavy metal freaks. I retreated into the corner and tried to hide my ukulele under my shirt.

Tables were moved back to accommodate the growing number of headbangers. Some air guitarists joined in. My beer was moving across the counter on its own, such was the volume. I didn't want to be there. I wanted to be out taking the evening air on the well-appointed and wide streets of Llandudno, then go back to my little room and watch *Newsnight*. This was bad karma coming back to haunt me because I had been facetious with the Christians earlier. I was about to be thrown to the lions.

One deafening last chord and the band finished, dropped their instruments and walked away without a word. The host looked round. 'Where's that ukulele player?' he called through the speakers. 'Tell him he's on next.'

'He means you,' said the big bloke I was trying to hide behind.

Life is a learning curve, I told myself as I walked to the stage. I would laugh at this in years to come. I got to the microphone and said, 'Are you ready to Uke?'

A desultory cheer. A table of tough-looking middle-aged women started a slow hand clap. A headbanger standing right in front of me said, 'Have you got a drummer?'

'No. Why?'

'I wouldn't worry about it.'

I started to play. The soundman turned me up to max. A man at the bar raised his glass to me and gave me the thumbs up. I didn't tell anyone, but I decided to dedicate my set to him.

I had three songs and I made sure every one of them was a rock-solid 12-bar blues; every one with a head-banging beat; every one in A, so that there was an almost seamless switch from one number to the next. Basically, I gave them as blistering a 15 minutes of R&B as it's possible to give when you've only got four strings.

I was getting into it. Thrashing about – a bit. And then I saw what I never thought I'd see: heavy-metal fans head-banging to my music. I was so shocked I stopped singing for a moment. I wanted to say, 'Excuse me. You do realize you're head-banging to a ukulele?'

I kept going, as fast as I could, focusing on the end of the song. I had just long enough to think: actually, this isn't going too badly, in fact, this is a good crowd; in fact, Wales has been the most welcoming part of the country I've been to.

I played the last chord of 'Route 66' – a deafening A7th. And got a much better response than I expected. I considered saying something affectionate like, 'People in Shropshire told me Wales was full of idiots, but it's not,' but I thought better of it and, instead, walked off stage with a sneer, in the way all the other bands had done.

An arm grabbed me before I could sneak out. 'Sorry,' I said instinctively. But it was the man who had given me a thumbs up at the start of my set.

'I play my ukulele in here sometimes,' he said. 'They love the ukulele here, don't they?'

'To a point.'

'You know what they really like?'

'AC/DC?'

'They like ballads. I played "Ain't She Sweet" once. They were all singing along by the end.'

I didn't believe it.

'Hang on … that might have been when I played at the folk club in Rhyl.'

I reckon if you played 'Ain't She Sweet' to this crowd you'd be found washed up on the beach in the morning.

He said, 'I want you to tell me where you got your kazoo holder from.'

'I made it.'

'But where did you get it from?'

'I made it myself. It's a coat hanger.'

I showed it to him and he was astonished. 'That's fantastic. Where can I buy one of these?'

'You can't buy them. You just get a coat hanger and twist it round.'

'Where did you get that idea from?'

I said, 'Here, have it.'

'I couldn't possibly. Where will you get another one?'

'The wardrobe.'

'God bless you.'

With one act of kindness my karma was restored.

Back at my B&B I found the hymn sheet in my pocket. I tried to play one of them on the ukulele, but I didn't know the tune. It didn't matter. My spirit had been saved. I could sleep the sleep of the just.

chapter eight

ferry cross the mersey

The train rattled back along the coast into England. The rain had returned and the low cloud obscured all views. Colwyn, Rhyl, Abergele – I didn't see any of them.

A man on the train insisted on pointing things out to me that weren't there. 'That's Southport across Liverpool Bay over there.' But all you could see was grey mist. 'And to your right you can see the Clwydian mountains.' But you couldn't, just more drizzle dribbling down the windows. He wasn't only talking to me. He tried to include the whole carriage. He had appointed himself unofficial guide. Maybe he was after tips.

'We've had no summer,' he said.

'Last couple of days were all right,' said the woman opposite. 'I got sunburnt.'

'Call that summer.'

I thought back to Worthing and all the retired folk in shirtsleeves, their skin brittle from the sun. Up here the weather, like the terrain, was less tame and the locals were in its grip. 'It's grim up North,' said our guide, and he looked around at people's faces hoping there were some Southerners on holiday who would laugh at his jokes, but no one did.

It may have been traditionally grim up North, but no one could say William Lever, 1st Viscount Leverhulme, didn't do his best to try to brighten things up. Lever Brothers were responsible for Sunlight soap and for Port Sunlight, the purpose-built garden village for the soap factory workers. The train to Liverpool stopped there and it was too convenient not to hop off.

Everything in Port Sunlight was on the doorstep. Not only could a worker see the factory from his house, there was also a school, concert hall, swimming pool, library, social clubs to meet up in, a church to worship in, all within five minutes' walk. In 1845 Benjamin Disraeli described the difference between rich and poor in England as 'two nations between whom there is no intercourse and no sympathy'. Lever, who grew up in Bolton, and saw first hand the squalor the working class had to live in, did everything he could to bridge the gap. 'There is more to life than work,' he announced as he opened the Lady Lever Art Gallery, aiming to widen the cultural horizons of his employees.

There was simply no need for any worker at the factory to ever venture out of Port Sunlight, and the houses were so well designed and to such a high standard that it must have been a wrench to ever leave the company. Which was exactly what Lever wanted, of course. His largesse wasn't entirely altruistic. He knew the value of a happy workforce.

Strolling around the village these days, it has a movie-lot appeal, as if it's one big set for a suburban soap opera. There's little noise. You wouldn't dare drop litter. Almost every building is listed. You can even rent one of the houses as a holiday home. Until 1980 only workers at the factory were allowed to live on the estate. Since then, most of the houses have been sold privately, but the Village Trust maintains a firm grip. It decides what you can plant in your front garden. It decides on your chimney pot style and what colour you can paint your exterior.

I wanted to speak to a local who would invite me in for tea and give me the latest gossip and an assessment of whether Port Sunlight was a suitable place for a community to prosper in the 21st century. But the only people visible were the maintenance crews, tending to the gardens. Not a net curtain twitched in any of the houses. If I wanted to speak to a resident, I suspect I would have had to apply in writing to the Village Trust.

There appeared to be a lively poetry and acoustic music scene on the Wirral and so I decided to stay the night there instead of going into Liverpool. A café advertised a 'poets and troubadours' event, but when I phoned, the woman refused to admit any such thing existed. I asked if there was anywhere else I could play and she said, 'How would I know that?' But she said it with such an attractive Liverpool accent I couldn't believe she was being rude. I phoned the number again in the hope someone else would answer, but I got the same woman and this time she was definitely being rude.

I went to the Birkenhead Central Library, to see if I could find somewhere else to play. It was a busy branch and I had to wait my turn for a computer. The threat of nationwide library closures had received a great deal of attention over the previous year. The very idea was appalling, but who was I to protest? I hadn't been a library member for years. And yet every time I visited one on this trip, I was amazed at just how well used they were.

They'd reinvented themselves over the period I'd been away. Now they were lively, even noisy places. Kids sat around for story time. There were 'Community Corners'. If you didn't have internet access, a local library was essential – many people came to scroll through the job market on the computers.

A few things haven't changed, of course. You still have to put up with the occasional nutter, like the man at the terminal next to me in Birkenhead, who seemed to be perfectly happy one minute typing away on Facebook, but then put his head in his hands and started to fume. He typed something and waited for a reply. Then he began to grunt like an animal. I honestly thought he was going to headbutt the computer. Or stab it. I asked him if he was all right, but he growled at me and clenched his fists. I was the most scared I'd been on the whole trip.

Apart from that little blip, Birkenhead Library was as welcoming as all the others, and I found an open mic in a pub called the Swinging Arm, down on the waterfront. 'Better get here early,' the barman said on the phone.

I found a place to stay in a B&B that was full of builders from Wolverhampton. They were converting a premises nearby into a call centre. They just assumed I was in a similar line of work. 'Electrician?' guessed one of them.

'No …'

'Everyone's an electrician these days.'

I could never tell people what I was doing. It just sounded too unlikely. I didn't think anyone would believe me, so I always tried to be vague.

'… I'm just passing through.'

That wasn't enough for him. 'On a job?'

'No, I'm seeing a friend.'

Now he was suspicious. What sort of friend was it who wouldn't put me up when I'd come all the way from Derbyshire to see him?

'He's not well.'

I was fabricating a sick friend because I couldn't tell these builders I was going round the country playing the ukulele.

When he discovered I was travelling by bus, he offered to drive me.

'It's okay.'

'Where does your friend live?'

'It's not far.'

The Swinging Arm was far. I walked miles through the most glamorous quarters of Birkenhead where waste ground featured heavily, as did cars on bricks. I found the pub down a backstreet. The exterior was painted black and red and on the door was a sign that read *No Tracksuits*.

It turned out to be a bikers' pub. I would have known this had I been familiar with the motorcyclist's lexicon – a swinging arm is a bike's rear suspension frame – but it was also clear from the two motorbikes parked on the stage.

In fact, there were more bikes in the pub than people. For somewhere that advertised itself as a live music venue, the Swinging Arm was a very quiet place that night. One barman, one customer. By walking in, I increased business 100 per cent.

'I've come for the open mic.'

The lad at the end of the bar, looked up, surprised. 'I wasn't expecting anyone.'

'It is tonight?'

'Yeah.'

'No one else here yet?'

'They've all gone to watch *Harry Potter*.'

He introduced himself as Ian. He said, 'Hang on. I'll go and get Dave. Dave's got the gear.' And he ran out.

I got a drink and sat down and felt annoyed with J K Rowling for stealing my audience. As if she was short.

The décor in the Swinging Arm was unlike any I'd ever seen in a pub before. Instead of fox hunting prints and toby jugs there were bits of motorcycle screwed to the walls. A big picture of Che Guevara hung on one side of the main bar. Photos of groups of hairy men standing by their Harley Davidsons on the other. It was the kind of pub that was probably at its best when it was full of people out of their heads.

And yet, you could forgive the Swinging Arm anything, because it had the most sensational view. From the big window running along one whole side of the room, there was a breathtaking vista of the River Mersey with the whole of the Liverpool night skyline spread along the northern shore. The cathedral looked fearsomely Gothic. The Liver Building stood with its chest out, floodlit; I wanted Spiderman to swing between the towers. After three weeks of country villages and well-preserved spa towns, this view looked electrifyingly metropolitan to me, as if I'd crossed the ocean and here was my first view of the New World.

Ian came hurrying back with Dave and they hauled in some kit. I realized they were doing this all for me and wanted to tell them not to worry. But they were committed now. They plugged in guitar and bass and were all set to go, except they had no audience apart from me. I wondered what time *Harry Potter* got out.

I sat at a table right in front of the stage. They played a song together and I applauded energetically and nodded wisely. They played another, slower number, and I tried to applaud in a different, more profound, way.

'You have a go now?' said Ian.

'You bet,' I said, and I meant it. At the beginning of the trip I would have found playing to no audience disconcerting, but now I knew it was an opportunity I shouldn't pass up.

Ian handed me his guitar.

'It's okay,' I said.

'What are you going to play?'

'I've got my ukulele.'

They hadn't seen it. I'd had it in a plastic bag for the rain, but now I pulled it out and for the first time they looked a little concerned. So did the barman. Frankly, I don't blame them. The Swinging Arm was a man's pub. The idea of having some liberal play the ukulele on the same stage that Slasher and the Chain-gang had smashed their way through Motörhead's back catalogue the previous weekend was a worrying one. They had a reputation to maintain.

I said, 'Don't worry, I've played the Cross Keys in Llandudno.'

This didn't impress them. I suspect they considered pulling the blinds or letting me play behind locked doors, but in the end they decided to risk it.

Playing to no audience is strangely liberating. You can take risks you wouldn't normally take. 'This next song is by George Orwell.'

I happily ran through my set, flanked by the twin motorbikes. And, of course, without any audience, I played everything absolutely perfectly; sang like Little Richard, remembered all the words, and the sound was good too. Unfortunately, the atmosphere was ruined towards the end when four customers walked in.

'"When I'm Cleaning Windows"', one shouted when he saw me, which was a disappointment in a place like Liverpool, renowned for its wit.

'Play something by Half Man Half Biscuit,' shouted another.

Later, I waited for a bus back to my B&B. I asked someone which number I should catch and he said, 'Are you a visitor?'

I admitted I was and he immediately slipped into the role of official Birkenhead Chamber of Commerce welcoming party. 'You stick with me. You'll be all right.'

When the bus pulled up, he ushered me on board and said proudly to the driver, 'Visitor to Birkenhead.'

As we travelled through town he pointed out the facilities: the swimming pool, the park, the discount carpet shop. He even introduced me to three friends who got on. 'Visitor to Birkenhead.'

'Really. First time?'

'Yes.'

'How are you enjoying your stay so far?'

'It's very nice.'

'It's his birthday on Saturday,' my guide poked his friend.

'I'm 52.'

'He's having a karaoke.'

And his friend burst into song, right there on the bus.

'A good voice,' I said.

'He could have been professional. On your right we have the late-night chemist.'

You got the feeling Birkenhead didn't get many visitors. But I was glad of the company and just listening to these people speak was a joy in itself. I thought the change in accents would stop surprising me after Welsh. What could beat that? But when a group of Liverpudlians got talking, it didn't sound like speech; it sounded more like a performance.

No city in Britain is more synonymous with music than Liverpool, and should you ever forget this, there are plenty of reminders. Just standing on the ferry quay at

Birkenhead, watching the *Royal Iris* edge towards the pier, I found myself humming 'Ferry Cross The Mersey'.

Across the water the twin towers of the Liver Building soared above all else. And today was a special day: its centenary. 'Let's just go and say happy birthday, shall we,' said a grandma to her little grandson. 'Just go and say hello.'

The boat sped across the river, riding the fierce current. The whole of the waterfront was dressed up for the birthday celebrations and the day had been chosen especially for the opening of the new Museum of Liverpool. 'I don't know why we need a new museum,' sighed the grandma. 'It's all changing. I don't like all these new buildings. I prefer the old ones.'

Presumably some people had said the same thing about the new Liver Building a hundred years ago. But she had a point; it must have been hard to keep pace with the changes on Liverpool's waterfront these days. Money had poured into the regeneration programme after the docks closed. The old brick warehouses were restored and converted. Brave new concrete and steel designs grew up around them. UNESCO awarded the waterfront World Heritage status, and anywhere that possibly could became a museum.

Liverpool's tourist credentials are good. The Beatles just keep on giving. They have their own museum, their own tour; the houses John Lennon and Paul McCartney grew up in are looked after by the National Trust. It doesn't seem to matter how much of The Beatles the world is offered, it still wants more.

The city also has a slave trade history, and that other major-league tourist endorsement, a *Titanic* connection – a very strong one too, the liner sailed out of Liverpool; a lot of the crew were local; the city mourned its sinking more than most.

And yet, somehow Liverpool sits awkwardly with tourism, and the way it has sacrificed everything to the heritage industry seems desperate. 'Our days of manufacturing are over,' the builders in the guesthouse had said to me the previous evening. 'We're a nation of service providers now.' Well, heritage was the all-purpose service, but wherever I went, in Liverpool or anywhere else, if I saw an old factory or a mill or a dockyard turned into a museum it always looked as if heritage had been lost rather than gained. The Liverpool Waterfront had made its mind up where its future lay, but I wondered if it was really sustainable. The Beatles had more responsibility riding on them in modern Liverpool than they ever had back in the sixties.

At least the new Museum of Liverpool was concerned with the living city as much as it was with the past. Here was a celebration of Scouseness to end all celebrations, and everyone was invited to the party.

Entrance was free for the grand opening, and there was a match-day crowd, keen to support this coming together of Liverpool's culture from the days of the Empire to *Brookside*. Great effort had been made to make it accessible to all: TV featured heavily, so did football, the pop culture, the legendary wit and guile. And there was an emphasis on belonging – on what it meant to be Liverpudlian.

The crowds edged their way round the galleries, recognizing themselves and their kind in all the archive footage. 'Don't know where they got the money for this from,' was a remark I heard more than once, and indeed it seemed astonishing that such a project could be completed in such austere times. You could only be pleased it had. There was a great spirit on display here, an indomitability that had seen Liverpool survive all the wars and sunken ships and stadium tragedies. This was still one of the poorest cities in Europe, but there was a communal pride throughout, a sense of 'we're all in this together'.

As I walked to Lime Street Station, I stopped at a chain café for a cup of tea.

'Large or regular?' said the lad.

'Regular.'

'Here look, I'll give you a large one, same price, don't tell anyone. Sod 'em all, eh?'

Yeah, let's stick it to the Man.

Of course, this generosity might have been because I was beginning to look like a homeless person. The sun on my face, my overgrown beard, my mucky trousers, they could easily give the impression I was spending more time outside than was good for me.

Bus drivers had waived fares before now. If I didn't have enough change for something in a shop, cashiers often sighed and let me off. 'Just give me what you've got,' said one, as I searched through my pockets.

When I got to Manchester I went and sat in Piccadilly

Gardens and watched a man go through a bin. He pulled out a Primark carrier bag with a pullover inside. He held it up, couldn't believe his luck. Then he looked round for someone to share his good news with and immediately identified me as a kindred spirit. 'Some people throw money away,' he said.

Manchester looked like it could afford it. The boom days of the cotton trade had long gone, but the handsome buildings remained. The vast, old red-brick warehouses still gave the city an Imperial air and there was a European feel to the centre that few cities in Britain could manage.

Even the buskers were international. A Tijuana band played on one side of the square, a guitarist sang in French on another. In the middle, a drummer played in his own language, attacking his kit with a fierce energy and making an alarming noise. He had a money box in front of him, but no one could get near it for fear of being deafened.

Manchester had musical pedigree: the Hallé Orchestra, the Royal Northern College, Chetham's School of Music. It had been a centre for classical musicians long before it became better known for Madchester and Oasis. It had good music shops as well. In one I was given a lecture on the art of the kazoo.

I knew that there was a range of kazoos to be had and that my plastic one was right at the bottom. I explained to the assistant I was thinking of upgrading and he produced a selection of models: plastic, metal, wooden.

'The metal one has an adjustable diaphragm, gets a deeper, firmer sound. The wooden model is more mellow, more understated, a kazoo player's kazoo.'

169

'How about plastic?'

He stroked his chin. 'Plastic is … perfectly acceptable in the right situation.' He meant it was for amateurs. All this time my kazoo had been holding me back. I bought the expensive metal one.

'You can get lessons if you're interested,' he said. I thought he was joking, but he pointed me to the shop's display of classified adverts, a musician's marketplace stuck to the wall.

You could learn to play any instrument you wanted in Manchester. There was a teacher advertising for everything from piano to triangle. A guy named Rami offered didgeridoo lessons with the emphasis on circular breathing. There was synthesizer tuition. Banjo classes. You could learn massage for musicians. Book a vocal coach. You could book a string quartet for your party or a Rolling Stones tribute band. And there it was: '*Tin whistle and kazoo lessons.*'

The wall was also a place for bands to recruit new members. '*Band seeks drummer.*' '*Lead guitarist seeks band.*' '*Drummer seeks band.*' The whole thing needed managing better, someone to put the drummer seeking a band in touch with the band seeking a drummer. No one was looking for a ukulele player, but I could start my own band right here. There was even a songwriter looking for work, and a sound engineer offering cheap studio time. And here was a flat to rent with other musicians, and an accountant specializing in music royalties. It was the whole package.

There were a number of open mics advertising as well, including one at the Salvation Army. The circuit was booming. I opted for the Iguana Bar on the Manchester Road. It had a reputation. It claimed that comedians and musicians you now saw on the TV had cut their teeth there.

I'd phoned my wife and asked her to meet me. I was within reach of home now, and she was going to come and hear me play and then take me back to my own bed.

'I can be your groupie for the night,' she said.

'Better get here early then.'

I had a quick go at busking in Manchester, simply because everyone else seemed to be doing it, and also I wanted to try my new kazoo. I sat on a wall in Piccadilly Gardens and played away. The kazoo sounded all right and the adjustable diaphragm allowed me to choose from a range of kazoo-ness. There was a problem, though. It made me dribble. I was kazooing away with a thread of spit running out of the end. It didn't look good, and I didn't seem able to stem the flow. I returned to my trusty old tooth-marked plastic model. I was an amateur and should be proud of it.

Busking made me feel uncomfortable. It was the money thing again. The first coin that dropped in my faded blue hat made me feel like I was depriving someone else. I packed up and never busked again.

The open-mic host at the Iguana Bar introduced himself as Crazy Horse. He wore a singlet and no shoes. He had a long grey ponytail and a deep tan and may have ridden into Chorlton-cum-Hardy bareback over the plains.

He shook his head as he showed me his list. Every slot was booked up until midnight. There was a reason for this, though. 'It's closing down at the end of the week.'

Business rates had done for the owner. He was calling it a day, so this was the last night of an open mic that had run for 10 years and all the stalwarts had turned out to play. 'Put your name down,' said Crazy Horse. 'See what happens.'

The bar may have been closing but Crazy Horse was determined it would go out in style. He reminisced on stage with the regulars.

'Remember when you set fire to your shirt?'

'Yeah, remember when you had to have your stomach pumped?'

'Good times.'

'The best.'

He gave all the acts a parting gift: a key ring with a Native American design on. 'I've got a whole load,' he said to me. 'Here, you can have one, for turning up.'

There was a range of performers unlike anywhere else I'd been. One man played some Delta blues on a cigar box guitar. Then he produced a broomstick bass, which had one string and made a noise like a plucked rubber band.

There was a lively poet who gave a vivid account of growing up on an estate in Manchester while she threw her arms around her head as if possessed.

And there was a father and daughter team who played their own home-made instruments. 'Hers is called a home-swinger,' said the father, and his daughter held up what a looked like a squat cricket bat with 12 strings and a sliding rod to alter the pitch. 'Mine is a chaoscillator,' he added and produced a battery-powered pad with six-inch nails in it and an oscillator.

They tuned up. The trouble was no one was really sure when the tuning up stopped and the performance started. It didn't matter. They made a sound you couldn't forget, no matter how hard you tried. A cross between the *Doctor Who* theme and water going endlessly down a plughole.

'We're going to miss you guys so much,' said Crazy Horse when they were through, and he gave them each a key ring.

This was all getting too emotional; the audience was going to be in tears soon. The next act saved us: a comic who decided that what we really needed to change the mood was 10 minutes of blazing misogynistic, racist, homophobic stand-up. 'Don't mind me,' he said. 'I just like to push the barriers.'

It was the only time I saw an open-mic crowd show genuine disapproval. They didn't boo or throw things or shout 'get off'. They just ignored him. The silence was withering. The man stood there, very alone. Then he turned and left the building. He didn't get a key ring.

My wife arrived. She hugged me and said, 'You don't smell so good.'

'That's life on the road.'

She looked nicely rested and healthy.

'That's life in Italy,' she said.

A duo called Daughters of Davis played. They were two sisters on tour in a van: busking, playing open mics, picking up what gigs they could find. They'd come up through the country like me; in fact, we'd played at some of the same venues. My wife said, 'They're on the road; they don't smell.'

She was right. They were 20 years old, all bouncy hair and puppyish energy. And they didn't smell. They'd packed up their jobs and were ready for the big time.

'We're going to miss the Iguana Bar and we've never played here before,' they told the audience, which was annoying because I had been planning on saying that if I got the chance. They set off at full throttle, one playing guitar, the other hitting a Cajon drum. They put muscle into their performance; every part of them contributed – their feet tapped, their hips swung, their eyelashes fluttered. When they sang you could see their uvulas quivering. Their only problem was they looked too nicely brought up, too wholesome to be successful. They needed a few tatts and some bags under their eyes. One of them said to me afterwards that she preferred open mics to proper concerts: 'If there's money involved everyone's dead competitive.' I believed her, but I suspect no one ever made it in the music business unless they secretly enjoyed trampling all over the competition.

Just before midnight Crazy Horse gave me the nod. It was way past my bedtime, but there was still a reasonable audience and they were very kind. I played my usual stuff and they all joined in, and then Crazy Horse started up behind me on the Cajon. Together we got the front row linking arms and swaying. 'This is great,' said Crazy Horse.

When I came to the end, he led the applause and I was about to step down when I heard the words 'More, more!'

I stood there like a rabbit in headlights. Crazy Horse prodded me. 'You've got an encore,' he said.

'I know.'

Even though I'd been waiting for the cry of 'encore' ever since Brighton, I hadn't got so carried away with the idea as to have something prepared. 'What shall I play?'

'Play an encore!'

So I played the song we always played as an encore in the Elderly Brothers: 'Great Balls Of Fire'. 'You shake my nerves and you rattle my brain ... bom bom bom bom.'

'I got an encore,' I said to my wife as we walked back to the car. 'I got an encore. Did you hear?'

'Yes. That was me.'

'Oh.'

The train bursts out of the Cowburn Tunnel into the Hope Valley and it's like the drugs have kicked in. The motorways and factories of Greater Manchester, where it always seems to be raining, are gone. Now the view out of the window is drystone walls and big wild hills, and it's not raining quite so much. The peat plateau of Kinder Scout looms to the north, the carpeted dales of Derbyshire roll to the south. The traveller is caught unawares and is immediately mugged by the Peak Park.

I was caught in the deep fashion-gulf between the passengers. Half were hikers dressed in ripped T-shirts and jeans and clutching beer bottles; half were going to the Tramlines music festival in Sheffield and were dressed in breathable membranes and gaiters.

Maybe it was the other way round.

I planned on enjoying both those activities that day, and as usual I had my ukulele on my back and was dressed in trousers you unzipped at the knee. But they were clean trousers for the first time in three weeks and my beard was trimmed, my shoes cleaned. I was rested after a couple of nights at home, and no longer looked like a vagrant.

'You're here, but you're not really here, are you?' my wife had said as we sat in the garden.

It might have been a mistake coming home. I didn't unpack. I couldn't relax.

'You don't feel like stopping now?' she said. 'Now you've proved your point.'

'The Smoo Cave Hotel is counting on me. They're probably printing the posters right now.'

I called the hotel on Cape Wrath, just to check I was still expected. A Scandinavian woman answered. She said she had heard I was coming. The manager must have already briefed the staff. They were probably busy thinking how they would cater for the audience, get extra help, maybe hire some more chairs. They'd probably tell the local press. The TV might be there.

'What instrument do you play?' she asked.

'Ukulele.'

'What?'

'Ukulele.'

'How do you spell it?'

I plotted a route north: through Yorkshire, up the northeast coast to Newcastle, then into Scotland. This was when I first saw Edinburgh on the map and realized I'd be getting there right at the start of the festival. I felt a little frisson. The Edinburgh Festival. I had always wanted to be part of the Edinburgh Festival; it was where every one-man show wanted to play. But what could I do there? I had no idea. All I knew was I would never have a better opportunity to do it.

'You got to live fast die young,' I said to my wife.

'You're too old to die young.'

I left the train at Hathersage to walk over the moors into Sheffield. The village was like a catwalk for hikers displaying their new equipment. Only the bravest took to the hills these days without a solar-powered packed lunch. And just how did we ever manage to go walking before ski poles became essential kit? We must have kept falling over all the time.

With steep slopes all around and the crags visible above, there was a Tyrolean feel to Hathersage, and yet we were no more than five miles from Sheffield and in the busiest National Park in the country. As I headed up towards Stanage Edge, a group of 42 ramblers passed me. I counted them. They just kept on coming, a crocodile of synthetic fibre.

The top was just as busy with rock climbers, and you could be forgiven for thinking that the Peak District was just one big outdoor pursuit centre. Nothing wrong with that, some would say. Access to these moors was hard fought for. Both of my parents grew up around Manchester in the 1930s, but had they taken the train out here, they wouldn't have been able to get anywhere near the places I was walking. In those days the moorland was all privately owned and kept for the annual grouse shoot. It took 30 years of campaigning and negotiating to create the National Park.

But there's another resource the Peak provides that's even more important than leisure or agriculture or anything else. And that's the wet stuff. Rainwater.

The water catchment of these uplands is enormous, big enough to supply the industrial and drinking water needs of Sheffield, Manchester and the East Midlands. A network of reservoirs controls the modern supply, but for hundreds of years the high rainfall up here has been driving industry below. As I came down towards Sheffield I passed through the Rivelin Valley on a trail that had me jumping across stepping stones and wading the river, with no clue I was anywhere near a large urban area. The path wound down past the remains of watermills, only millponds and stone foundations poking through the brambles now, but back in the 18th century the forges and grinding wheels that powered Sheffield's growing cutlery industry were at work in the cool glades of this valley, all fuelled by water from the moors.

The first sign of the city was a few allotments; then a playground and café, and then I came up from the river bank and there was Hillsborough and a tram stop.

Two women waited, clutching Sainsbury's Bags for Life. 'On a Wednesday he goes to the Northern General for his eyes. On Thursday it's the Hallamshire for his heart. On Friday he goes to the Claremont for his breathing, and then on Monday back to the Northern General for his knees.'

Sheffield's Tramlines Festival was such an unlikely concept it seemed too good to be true. It sounded like the result of the day the city council had a meeting and someone slipped something into the tea. 'I know, for one weekend each year, let's turn Sheffield into one big concert venue with lots of different stages spread all over the city centre.'

'Yeah!'

'And let's make it all free!'

'Yeah!'

They all voted in favour and by then it was too late.

The result was 125,000 people taking to the streets for a musical bash that was just the right side of chaos. There was a world music stage, a new music stage, folk stage, dance stage, youth stage, an unannounced stage, all squashed into any space available throughout the city. Add to this makeshift stages in every bar, pub, sports centre and art gallery and there was no escape. If you jumped on a bus, you were confronted by a card-carrying busker.

I was looking for the folk stage where I'd been told there was an open-mic opportunity. It had been pushed away out of sight in a park, as if the sensibilities of the folk crowd couldn't cope with the carnage of the main festival. In a sylvan setting a stage had been erected, and on the grass a small, laid-back crowd was listening to a young woman from Bury.

'This isn't really a folk song,' she said, which seemed like a dangerous thing to say at a folk concert, but she played and sang in a dreamy way that was perfect for a summer's afternoon.

I couldn't believe they would let just anyone up there to play, and of course I was right. This wasn't the open-mic stage. This woman had been booked, was being paid. She had CDs for sale.

I asked one of the many people in hi-viz jackets where the open mic was and he directed me back to the entrance. I'd missed it because it wasn't so much a stage as a gazebo with four tent pegs keeping it from blowing away. There was no audience because the audience was all listening to the woman with the CDs for sale. But there was a microphone and a little amp, and a very keen soundman.

'You want to play?'

'I don't know.'

'Go on. It'll be great.'

'There are no people.'

'There were no people when the last band started but they had a crowd by the end.'

I was backtracking. 'Thing is, I don't know any folk music.'

'They'll love a ukulele. Everyone loves a ukulele. Please. I haven't had anyone play for ages.'

He was begging me. What could I do? I plugged in and he sound-checked me. 'You're set. All yours.'

I started playing to the shrubs. The first thing that happened was the soundman disappeared. The second thing was that he was right, a crowd did start to form. But this rather worried me. They'd come to hear folk music and all I was going to do was annoy them.

I played a Leadbelly song, 'Midnight Special', which was kind of folky, and they clapped politely. But that was all I knew. So I said, 'The blues is folk music really, isn't it?' and I played my Blind Willie McTell number. That went down okay, so I said, 'Since we're playing the blues, here's a Chuck Berry song,' and within two bounds I was back playing my normal set.

A man in a suit started to twist himself in a way that might just have been classified as dancing. A couple on a tandem pulled up to watch. A traffic warden stopped and listened. A woman called out, 'You know any Buddy Holly?' You bet. I played 'That'll Be The Day' and she and her friend got up to jive.

The soundman came back with a cup of tea. 'See, I told you you'd get an audience. You can finish after this one.'

'Why? It's going well.'

'Someone else wants to play.'

An eight-year-old took over from me. She sang a song from *The Lion King* and brought the gazebo down.

As I left, the man in the suit came up to me and said, 'Well done; you're spreading the word.'

'What word?'

'The rhythm and blues word. You're converting people. Man.'

I went back into the city centre. It had become a muggy, smoggy brown evening. Everyone walked round clutching a drink in each hand, and the streets were knee-deep in lager cans and burger boxes. The pubs were bulging. Music was being pumped out of every building into the street, and from the street more music was being pumped back into the buildings again.

Such was the proximity of everything to everything else it was hard to hear, so sound engineers used that old trick of turning everything up louder. I caught one band called Danananananaykroyd, who were billed as a Glaswegian party-starting, fight-pop band with two frontmen and two drummers. I thought: this is going to be so loud it shouldn't be missed. But when I got there, there was only one drummer. Outrageous. I felt cheated.

It was all one big assault on the senses. People were behaving as though they'd gate-crashed a party and were determined to have as wild a time as they could before they got chucked out. As darkness fell and the sea of bottles and cans grew deeper, the city edged towards bursting point. There was an alcohol-fuelled tension that could have kicked off any minute.

A lad had a pint of beer poured over his head. He stood there dripping and said, 'I wish Sheffield was like this every weekend.'

chapter nine

yorkshire folk

I was walking beside the Leeds and Liverpool Canal, lost in a recurring fantasy: I've been invited on the Jools Holland show, *Later*, and Jools is interviewing me at the piano, as he does, asking me questions about my life in music.

'So tell us, Mark, how did the Elderly Brothers take it when you set off to pursue your own career?'

'They were furious, Jools.'

'Really?'

'Well, I did have the beer kitty ... But, seriously. They understood. We'd taken the band as far as we could.'

'And what inspired you to hit the road with a ukulele and handful of songs?'

'I guess I wanted to get back to my roots. Get closer to the audience.'

'And as I understand it you were talent-spotted at an open mic in Rotherham?'

'That's not true ... it was Doncaster.'

Jools laughs. The audience laughs. 'One last question,' he says. 'You've become a success somewhat later in life than most musicians. Was there ever a time when you thought it might never happen, when you almost gave up?'

'Yes Jools, there was.' And then I tell him this story.

It was July 2002, the annual children's concert held in the hall in the Derbyshire village where I live.

Parents were encouraged to support their children at these events, of course, but I decided to take it a level further by suggesting to my boys, then 10 and 12, that I play with them, that we form a guitar trio.

I picked a Fernando Sor piece with three parts and insisted for the month before that they came up to my study every evening after school to rehearse. Not for their sake, of course – they could read the music and they quickly picked it up; the intense rehearsal schedule was because I could only play the piece by heart, and because my part had to play the opening two bars solo. 'Why don't we just wing it?' said the eldest, as I introduced extra rehearsals the week before the big night. Wing it? I didn't like the sound of that at all. I would only be happy when I could play the piece like a robot.

By the night of the performance we were note perfect. We sat and watched the other acts perform, children playing violin and piano while their parents turned the pages or watched from the front row playing every note themselves.

When our turn came, we took to the stage and composed ourselves. I nodded to the boys and set off on my solo opening bars. And that was when my brain blanked.

I got a few notes out, but then seized up and stopped. I laughed nervously, the audience laughed nervously with me. 'We'll just try that again,' I said.

I tried again and exactly the same thing happened. I simply couldn't remember what to play.

A panic was rising in me. My hands were sweating. When I glanced round at the boys, they looked back at me very strangely. I felt trapped, chained in a box like Houdini, padlocks and straitjacket confining me, and the clock ticking as the water level rose and I desperately tried to fight my way out.

It was at that moment I promised myself that if the powers that be could help me get out of this village hall with any dignity left, I would give up the whole crazy notion of being a musician and never pick up another instrument again.

I had another go. Same result. I smiled again. The audience smiled again. They were being very sympathetic. And that was when I realized that they had no idea this was my fault. They thought it was all the boys'. How could I be to blame? I was the responsible adult, the steady hand steering the little ones along. I wasn't messing up the intro. They weren't coming in on time.

My treachery began there. Instead of admitting guilt I happily let my children take the blame. I said to them, so the audience could hear, 'I think we can play it a little better than that, don't you?' My eldest looked at me with a 'What the ...?'

With the pressure on me reduced, I tried once more. This time I just lunged at it. I probably didn't play anything on the page except the note just before the boys' cue. That was enough. They grabbed it and they were away. They took my hand and led me to the end of the piece.

I did feel ashamed afterwards. So ashamed it was hard to push the boys behind me and accept all the applause, although I did it anyway, and it's worth noting that by that time I had completely forgotten the promise I had made to quit music.

This memory had been triggered by a children's concert poster on the notice board of a village hall I'd just passed. It often crept up on me like that, and whenever it happened I was amazed at how I still cringed with guilt and longed to confess. Was it because I had muscled in on my children's moment in the spotlight? Or was it because I had reneged on a promise?

It was neither of those things. It was because in a similar situation I'm sure I would do exactly the same thing again.

The canal was never far from a main road, yet there was always a feeling of seclusion. I was heading towards Skipton, coming into town through the side entrance, past back gardens of all descriptions: some with gnomes and hanging baskets; some fitted out with Homebase decking, outdoor heating fans and a barbecue the size of a blast furnace; others left to wilderness. One man was working away on his plot, cutting back undergrowth. 'Make a nice allotment,' I said. 'South-facing.'

'I'm building a car port,' he told me.

School holidays had begun, but the canal was so empty of traffic you wondered how the boat hire companies ever did any business. The only boats I saw were privately owned, beautifully kept and looking as though they never went anywhere. A big dog jumped out of one very smart barge and charged up to me. A woman stuck her head out of the cabin and called the animal back. 'I'm sorry. You wouldn't believe how well behaved he is in obedience classes.'

Her narrowboat was called *Merryweather* and was spotless with all the ropes coiled into neat circles on the deck. A disobedient dog didn't fit with her lifestyle. 'You can buy zappers, you know,' she said.

'Zappers?'

'Electric collars. You have a remote control and if they run off, you zap them.'

A man came out onto deck. He emptied a dustpan over the side. I wasn't sure if he was husband or staff. He shook his head. 'You can't go round zapping the dog.'

'It's not high voltage or anything. Just a gentle zap.'

He sighed and went back inside. The zapper conversation was one they'd had before. He knew if the dog got one, he'd be next.

My folk music experience in Sheffield had been heartening and I was feeling positive as I arrived in Skipton where I planned to play at a folk club.

In the past when I'd been to these evenings I'd always got the feeling there was a code of conduct I was unaware of; I might laugh at something that wasn't supposed to be funny and sit on my own for the rest of the evening. I was still concerned about having no real folk music in my repertoire, but the audience at the Tramlines Festival hadn't minded. And folk music had never been more mainstream. I was sure Skipton would be gentle with me.

The club met in a pub called the Narrow Boat, right on the canal. But when I went in, I found an empty bar. 'Folk night?' said the barman.

'That's right.'

'Bottom of the back room there's a door. Through there and up the stairs.'

This did nothing to allay my fear of a secret society. I went up the stairs and got to a door. I could hear singing. I waited until it had finished and walked through. A room full of eyes turned to me. I sat down quietly. How could I convince them I wasn't the secret police? The club secretary coughed and waved a book of raffle tickets at me. I bought a whole strip. It was a brilliant move; from that moment I was in.

A guitarist played a song of unrequited love. The interesting thing about it being you could hear every note and every word he sang. This was partly because there was no background noise – no pool table or Sky Sports; no one on their phone. But there was something else, and it took me a moment to realize what. There was no amplification. It was just him, his voice and his guitar, the first purely acoustic setup I'd come across.

I asked if I could be put on the list. The host said, 'One song be all right?'

'Sure.'

'They're all back from university. They all want to play.'

There was a family feel to the evening as two youngsters rattled off a flute and violin jig. A guitarist played some Jake Thackray songs. A girl sang a sad Irish ballad in which everyone died horribly.

When my spot came it was just so strange to have an audience listening so keenly. In fact, it felt a little intimidating. I made a rotten chord change and everyone in the room flinched.

I played the Lead Belly tune 'Midnight Special'. I was fooling no one about my folk roots, but there was a holiday spirit in the audience and they were singing the chorus by the end.

An *a cappella* group did a couple of numbers, and then a guitar and mandolin duo. It was all good stuff, although the highlight of the evening was still to come: the raffle.

This was a fixture, and while they didn't take the music too seriously on a singers' night like this, the same couldn't be said about the raffle. It would have happened whether anyone had turned up to play or not. In fact, Skipton looked like one of those places where there's a bye-law that if more than five people are gathered together it's compulsory to have a raffle.

There were two prizes, both wrapped. 'There's a square prize and round prize tonight,' said the raffler. 'And there's a bottle of vin red.'

'I wouldn't choose the wine if you win,' said my neighbour.

I know this trick. Whoever wins the wine re-donates it to the next raffle. It's a brilliant means of income generation. A £3 bottle of wine from the Co-op can raise £500 over a couple of years. It only stops earning when someone accidently drinks the thing.

'Remember,' said the raffler as he shook up the bag of tickets, 'if you don't like your prize, give it back.'

He called out the numbers. I didn't win, thank goodness. It doesn't do for a visitor to win a local raffle. The round prize turned out to be a tin of biscuits. The square prize was … another tin of biscuits. It took a while for the audience to settle down after the excitement. There was another half hour of music to come, but with the raffle over it was all a bit of an anticlimax.

'Morning!' said the man in the Leeds United shirt as he strode past. A bold, unequivocal Northern 'good morning' with eye contact and a grin full of dodgy teeth; none of the weak-livered, eyes-to-the-ground mumble that you got as an after-thought down South.

This was true-grit Yorkshire and I was walking from Bolton Abbey to Ilkley through Wharfedale, following the river downstream. Cool peaty water rushed at my side and up ahead were the slopes of Ilkley Moor. How North Country was that?

But then Ilkley turned out to be nothing like it should have been. Just the name made you think: wet, foggy, grim. But here it was preparing for its summer festival, basking in occasional sunny periods and choking with petunias.

Only at the town's tennis club, where there was a junior tournament in progress, was there anything like some Yorkshire gristle on display, as a team of heavily trained youngsters worked on their bad sportsmanship. The girls tuned their grunts to high volume. The boys had learnt how to curse to a professional level. And they all had the potential to be really good at racket abuse. I didn't dare crunch on my apple in case I caused a distraction and got shouted at by a 14-year-old. One girl volleyed a ball into the net and screamed, 'For God's sake, Charlie! What's wrong with you?' I could have told her, but she wouldn't have liked it. I took to the hills.

I'd done pretty well so far without a map. I'd kept to rivers and canals and well-worn paths. I'd not been an adventurer. But now up on Ilkley Moor, I lost my bearings.

I was heading for Chevin beacon, but one beacon looks like another in unfamiliar country and I found myself walking in a circle. I got caught in a marshy patch. I was all alone on Ilkley Moor, surrounded by bog, and overhead the jets from Leeds Bradford Airport were circling.

I came across a barn and asked for directions from a farmer working in the yard. I expected a reply in broad Yorkshire, but he answered in broad cockney, 'Where you wanna get to?'

'Harrogate.'

''Arrogate. Blimey. What you want to go there for?'

I wanted to say, 'I'm playing the ukulele in a bar called Katana.' But once again I bottled it. 'I'm seeing a friend.' At least the friend wasn't sick any more.

'What's the address?'

'I'm ... not sure.'

'You don't know the address?'

'They live near WH Smiths.'

He directed me down the hill into a village where, within 10 minutes, a bus with the magic word 'Harrogate' on the front came along. I found a newspaper on the seat and on the front page was an advert for a weekend break in Edinburgh, *The World's Festival City*.

'Harrogate is the queerest place with the strangest people in it, leading the oddest lives of dancing, newspaper reading and dining.'

So said Charles Dickens when he came to the town in 1858. In those days Harrogate made the most of its spa epithet, promoting itself as the place you came to be seen in the fashionable North. By the turn of the 19th century it was a celebrity parade, drawing the elite from all over Europe. The local newspaper produced a who's who of people visiting each week.

'If there's one thing you should do while you're in Harrogate,' said the woman who ran my B&B, 'it's go and have an ice cream at the parlour in Valley Gardens.'

That sounded like good local advice, so I went there and sat on a bench, licking a mint and chocolate chip cornet. I was wearing sunglasses, partly for the sun, partly because the flowers were so colourful. 'It's the water,' said a gardener, 'stuffed with minerals, they last all summer.'

Health and longevity were what Harrogate was built on. I started reading the names of the dedicatees on the park benches to see how long they'd lived. Peter Blades, 74 – not so impressive. Robert Hemsley, 85 – better.

This sort of pastime wasn't good for me. I clutched my ice cream and felt uncomfortably in touch with my own mortality. In an effort to illustrate that death is as much a part of life as birth, fate sent six women pushing prams through the gardens at speed. What strange sort of competition was this? Were they mothers or nannies? Maybe it was Rag Week. None of those: the ice cream parlour was about to close.

I found the Katana Bar, but at eight o'clock it still hadn't opened, and from the outside looked closed for good. The chairs were on the tables. A poster in the window advertised an event long gone. The only sign of life was the over-flowing cigarette bin on the wall, the butts littered all over the pavement.

I wandered round town and came across the Blues Bar which had an open mic, but on a different night. A shame. It looked like a good venue. Through the window I could see an energetic guitarist playing to a small but attentive audience, and I was tempted to go in and put my feet up and spend the evening there.

I went back to have one last check on the Katana Bar, and this time it was open, although the word 'open' didn't really do justice to the indifference of the place. A few people were standing outside smoking. Inside, the chairs were being taken off the tables, and a lad was setting up his sound equipment. It didn't look encouraging; still, I asked him if I could play.

'Play what?'

'Ukulele.'

His curled lip said: if you really have to.

I counted the audience: five. Make that three, as two of them went outside to stand by the cigarette bin. They were young, twenty-something, which was fine with me, but explained why there was no beer behind the bar, just lager. The barman said, 'Draught's off, only bottled. Three for a fiver.'

'I'll just have one.'

'It's three for a fiver.'

'I don't want three. I just want one!'

'But you get three. It's a deal. Have one now, and come back twice more. They'll be like free ones.'

'I can't drink that many.'

'It's only three.'

'Yeah, but I don't like the stuff.'

'For a fiver.'

'Just give me one.'

He gave me one. It cost £3.50.

The host played a few songs. The Katana was a very small bar, but the volume was cranked up so high and with so much treble, his guitar sounded like an amplified dental drill.

Which was how just the audience liked it. So what did I know?

He handed over to me. Buoyed by my experience in Skipton the previous evening I said, 'Can I suggest something radical?'

'What?' He was going to say no, whatever I said.

'We turn off the amp.'

'Turn off the ...?' He looked appalled. 'You don't want to do that.'

'There are only five people in the room. There's no need for a mic. It'll be all right. Trust me.'

'You got to have a microphone.'

'Why?'

'It wouldn't be an open mic if you didn't, would it?' And he put the microphone right in front of me. He didn't want any trouble from uppity ukulele players. 'We like it amplified, all right.'

They were a bit suspicious of me now. It was the first time on the trip that my age made me feel conspicuous.

I played 'Roll Over Beethoven'. The audience briefly swelled to six as three came in from having a smoke, but then dropped to four as two went out to take their place. There was always someone out there. The host took his turn, so did the barman. It was as if they had to keep the fire burning. Maybe it was a charity smoke.

I hurried through my songs. They weren't totally unimpressed. I think even the host warmed to me in the end. 'Tell you what,' he said, 'come back when it livens up and play again.'

It was 10 o'clock by now. 'Come back when?'

''Bout two.'

I went back to the Blues Bar and caught the end of the featured guitarist's set. He played self-penned songs with a rich voice and guitar style honed over the years. It wasn't blues, it wasn't folk. He was just a guy who knew what he was doing and had confidence in his material. He had the audience on his side, and he looked pleased with his evening's work, but the more I listened to him the more I thought: an open-mic performer gets more value out of a good performance than someone like this does.

When a professional performs he generally expects things to go to plan. He knows what will work and what won't; he's used to being in control. When the audience applauds at the end and calls for more, it's satisfying, but it's business as usual.

There's no such thing as business as usual for the average open-mic player. The only thing he is used to is the thrill of the unknown. He might open his case and discover he's left his instrument at home. He has no idea what he's going to sound like, or what the audience response will be. His performance is a tightrope walk during which he could easily play one song and sing another. His only chance of going crowd surfing is if he trips over his guitar lead.

Imagine then, the blast he gets when, by some fluke, things go right: he remembers to plug into the amp; he doesn't lose his plectrum inside his guitar; he doesn't chip his front teeth on the microphone; the four people in the audience not only listen to him, they cheer and clap, and the host is so impressed he gives him a free drink and asks him back the following week. He may be playing on a quiet Monday in the back room at the Old Nag, but if he closes his eyes he's centre stage at a sold-out Madison Square Garden.

The following morning I turned up at the Royal Pump Room to take the waters. Celia Fiennes, whom I'd last encountered in Bath, did the same thing when she visited Harrogate on another side-saddle journey in 1697. She wrote: 'The smell being so very strong and offensive I could not force my horse near the well.'

She wasn't exaggerating. The Royal Pump Room was built over the original sulphur well, but an outside tap still produces the water. I pressed the button and it gurgled and rumbled and then spewed forth a fountain of the most evil-smelling black liquid. You weren't expected to drink this surely?

Two motorcyclists appeared. 'What's it taste like?' asked one. He was Australian.

'I don't know,' I said.

'Guidebook says it's the strongest tasting well water in Europe,' and he shoved the book at me to prove it.

He pressed the button in the wall, and the tap spluttered into his hand. He smelt it, let his friend smell it, then said, 'Bottoms up!' and took a gulp. 'Mmm. Rotten eggs,' he said, as if he was reviewing it. 'Sulphur.'

His friend tried it. 'Sulphur is very good for you. Good for the skin. Gets rid of poisons.'

I had to try some now. I filled my hand and slurped it up. It was so strong it tasted of meat. I tasted it again. Actually, it wasn't too bad.

The curator at the Royal Pump Room Museum said to me, 'To get the full effect you need to slug it back like vodka, but taste it like Bollinger.'

He offered me a glass. When I told him I had just tried some outside he said, 'The water in the tap outside is for lightweights; this is the strong stuff.'

It didn't taste any different, and I wondered if the wealthy visitors of the past really believed in the efficacy of sulphur baths, peats baths, wax baths, or whether they just came to Harrogate because it was a good place to network.

'The sulphur waters are good for digestion,' said the curator. 'A pint of this will cure constipation overnight.'

I was beginning to get a distinct whiff of snake oil.

Before I left Harrogate I visited Bettys Tea Rooms. In the Imperial Room they were dining and reading newspapers just like Dickens had said. If only they had been dancing, it could have been 150 years ago.

'I don't normally travel by bus,' said a woman on the way to Rippon. 'My husband's taken my car to work – his is being serviced. I can't remember when I last travelled by bus.'

She spoke as if she was embarrassed, that bus travel was for the less well-off. But I was so used to it by now, I treated a bus as if it was home, and I'd almost forgotten what it was like to have car keys in my pocket. I was familiar with the layouts of the different buses and I found I always took the same seat: on single deckers the first row of the raised seats towards the back – kerbside as a preference; on double deckers I could never resist the top deck front seat if it was free.

People moaned about the length of the journeys; they sat there stoically. But I had all day, and I liked it when we went round the houses. A tour of an estate told me things about a town a guidebook didn't cover. And if you found a newspaper on the seat and read how new mum Charley Stickley who works at Sainsbury's had been crowned Carnival Queen, well, it made you feel like a native.

I felt as though I'd been travelling in Yorkshire for days, but here I was only just reaching York. I went straight to the tourist office to enquire if there was a lunchtime concert anywhere.

The assistant didn't look optimistic. 'Don't think so. It's a bit late now anyway.'

'It's lunchtime.'

'There's nothing on the notice board.'

'How about in a church? They often have lunchtime concerts in churches.'

She searched on her computer. I could see the screen from where I was standing. 'No,' she said. 'There's nothing.'

'What's that?'

'What?'

'This harp concert. In St Martins.'

'Oh yes.'

'Where's St Martin's?'

'Just round the corner. Starts in two minutes. You'll have to hurry.'

I ran round to St Martins. The harpists were poised, first harp string about to be plucked. As soon as I sat down in a pew, they were off.

I'd never seen a harp quartet play before; I didn't know there could be such a thing. It didn't take long for me to decide that this was the nearest you could get to hearing the soundtrack to heaven. When they played a Bach fugue I closed my eyes and felt a weightlessness that I'm not sure was good for me.

They were four young women, straight out of music school, and they called themselves the Clouds Harp Quartet. They were actually on tour, on much the same route as I was, from North Wales to Manchester to York and on to Edinburgh. 'We're going to feel jolly tired after this month,' said one of them. Well, I bet they were if they each had to cart a harp round. I complained if I had to carry a bag of apples extra in my rucksack.

They played a suite called *Clouds*, written by one of the players, which was dreamy and unrestrained as they went through the whole range of clouds from wispy cirrus to thundery cumulonimbus. They improvised in places and incorporated poetry, and the piece was so carefree it was as if it was caught on a breeze.

Afterwards the small audience responded politely as audiences always do in a church. We wanted to call for more but wondered if we were allowed, until one of the quartet said, 'We know another one if you like.'

Maybe that was the only way I would get an encore, just announce I was going to do one.

They played us a folk song. And I would suggest that the experience of hearing a harpist play and sing at the same time is something we should all try to have before we die. Maybe as we die.

It's a guess, but I would say this was the only harp quartet concert in the whole of Britain that day, and Clouds really deserved better publicity and a bigger audience. But making a living as a harp player is, I'm sure, tougher than it looks. I saw one of them later in the afternoon, her harp now zipped up in a huge padded bag and fixed to a sort of golf trolley. She was pushing it across the cobblestones of Olde Yorke, probably heading out to the bypass, to hitchhike a ride to Edinburgh.

York was at the opposite end of the visitor attraction scale to Birkenhead, and was a battleground for tourist guides who tirelessly corralled their charges with their coloured umbrellas held high. I didn't see a fight break out, but I bet they weren't uncommon, as visitors from all nations pushed and shoved their way round the Minster and down the Shambles.

I found myself forever stepping into photographs. Or being asked to take photographs. One Chinese family handed me their camera and asked me to take a shot of them with the Minster in the background. I took the picture, but when the father scrolled back to look for it, it was clear it hadn't worked. He asked me to take another. That didn't work either. His wife was getting annoyed with him. 'Too much on the memory,' she said, and they argued about which pictures to delete. The kids sighed; the mother apologized. Finally she gave me her phone to take the photo. I managed it at last, and they thanked me greatly and one of the children offered me a piece of Minster fudge.

The city depended on its tourists and was very protective of them. I saw posters in cafés and souvenir shops protesting over the proposed closing of the coach park in town. I thought I'd read them wrong – normally we protest over the opening of a coach park. But these local businesses didn't want their valuable tourists deposited somewhere else. They wanted them right in the middle of the city where they could keep a grip on them.

I escaped to the river, where people sat with their feet dangling over the quayside, watching the Canada geese paddle to and fro. The thing about cities like York and Oxford is they transcend their tourists. The buildings are so old and sturdy that they look down on all the fuss as just a passing phase. They have so much history ingrained within them that they make everything else feel insignificant. I came across one old house in York with a plaque on it that read: *Here lived John Goodwick who discovered how to measure the universe.* A café advertising baked potatoes with 25 different fillings can't seriously compete with that.

The Minster stood in the middle of it all like a cultural power station, the beating heart of the city from which all light and energy emanated. As the sun dropped, the stone turned pink and it seemed to come alive and throb like an alien ship.

I found a place to stay a little way out of town. The woman of the house told me if I went out in the evening she'd like me back by 11 o'clock.

'I might be later than that.'

She looked at me with pinched lips, wondering what I could possibly be doing in York that would keep me out past 11. I decided to tell the truth this time. 'You see, I'm playing the ukulele in a bar and I might not get a slot until late.'

I might as well have told her I was meeting someone to buy heroin. '11.30, then.'

She took me upstairs and said, 'I'll show you how to work the toilet.'

It was a complicatd system, needing a demonstration.

'Flush, hold, slow release,' she said. 'Got that?'

'Flush, hold, release.'

'No. *Slow* release, or it won't work.'

'Slow release.'

We stood there and waited for the cistern to fill. 'Now you have a go,' she said.

I had a go. It wouldn't work.

'Flush, hold, slow release,' she repeated.

We waited for the cistern to fill again. I had another go. It half worked.

'Shame you're not staying longer,' she said. 'Takes a couple of days to get used to it.'

There were Morris dancers in town that night. I could hear them always just round the corner, their bells ringing, their sticks clattering. I think I have a fear of Morris dancers, if there is such a thing. I imagine they're going to pass a spell on me and my offspring. It's all the green man, fertility stuff that gives me the creeps. I tried to avoid them. I nipped into a pub that advertised itself as *The Most Haunted Pub in York*, and I felt considerably less spooked in there.

The pub also advertised an open mic, but it seemed low key to the point of comatose. There was one man with a guitar and no equipment, which should have suited me fine, but this place had so many alcoves and corners, you needed some volume. He saw my ukulele and asked if I wanted to play. 'Maybe,' I said.

'Suppose you're booked in somewhere else are you?'

The truth was that York was like an open-mic festival. There were at least four places to choose from that night and he'd seen through my plan – I was doing the rounds to see which one suited me best. But he must have been used to this. I felt sorry for him. I said I'd come back later.

He gave a nod – yeah, they all say that.

And he was right, of course. The second place I went to was called the Habit (as in nun's) and it was clear this was the place to be. It was that perfect mix of small, lively and diverse. I just managed to get on the long performers' list and stood back to hear probably the best music I'd heard so far. The pick was a handsome young singer-songwriter with a very powerful voice who had his own fan club in. They looked like they wanted to tear him apart and eat him.

I had to go on straight after, but I wasn't complaining. I was just pleased to be part of it. The audience threw their arms in the air for everyone. At 11 o'clock a band somehow squeezed themselves onto the stage, and got the place hopping. And that was when I had to leave.

What sort of rock 'n' roll tour was it when you had to be back in your digs at 11.30 or your landlady would lock you out? What about the orgies and the choking on your own vomit? As I walked under the city walls, two girls hurried past me, dressed up and heading into town. I heard one say, 'I'm not going to have sex tonight.'

Makes two of us, darlin'.

Back at the B&B I used the bathroom. The flush wouldn't work. I tried it three times, but it wouldn't catch. As I opened the door she was there.

'Did you release slowly?'

'Yes. Promise.'

She shook her head. 'Oh, go on. I'll do it.'

chapter ten

the wind cries newcastle

I was getting tired of places proving to be utterly unlike the way I imagined them to be. Filey was nothing but a grey holiday camp with a muddy shoreline and a caravan shanty town. Wasn't it? I'd spent 45 years thinking it was. So what was it doing being a pretty seaside resort, with impressive cliffs and views all the way down to Flamborough Head? I kept checking signs to make sure I was in the right place. I hadn't got off the bus too early had I? No, this was definitely Filey.

'Where's Butlins?' I asked in the tourist office.

'Closed in 1980-something.'

I went and sat on the big sandy beach and watched the families playing cricket and flying kites, and I wondered why I'd never brought my kids here. Because it was supposed to be nothing but a grey holiday camp with a muddy shore, that was why. Maybe I had been thinking of Skegness.

I took my shoes off and walked along the water's edge. Nowhere is the true Brit more at home than on the beach. The beach belongs to everyone. Rich and poor, fat and thin, everyone can be themselves. A little girl dropped her egg roll on the sand and her mum screamed at her. Her dad laughed and the girl gave the roll to the dog. Not five yards away a couple with Tupperware sat reading their Kindles quietly.

I bought some dressed crab from a seafront stall and headed off along the coast path.

I followed this cliff-top trail, the Cleveland Way, for the next three days. First to Scarborough, where the great arc of the bay came into view a good two hours before I got there. It was tucked under a castle-capped headland and seemed to be the most perfectly positioned seaside town. J M W Turner came here and made many drawings. The coast path took me right past the point where he sketched *Scarborough Town and Castle: Morning: Boys Catching Crabs*. And that's one painting not three.

Filey had just been an hors d'oeuvre of a resort; Scarborough was the main course, with steamers offering trips round the bay; donkey rides along the beach; deckchairs to rent for £2; and more fish and chip shops than a town deserves.

I walked in past the Spa, the grand entertainment centre along the front, to find Howard Beaumont, 'King of the Keyboard', playing the organ to a mature audience. They were sitting in the Sun Court, which was open-air but enclosed behind perspex screens, which I assumed were to act as windbreaks, but in reality frazzled the poor dears like insects under a magnifying glass.

A banner read *Tap your toes to a vast repertoire of showstoppers and easy listening*. Howard Beaumont was playing with great verve and whenever he gave the audience something they recognized, the toe tapping turned into clapping and singing along. They would have held up their lighters had there not been a smoking ban.

There was probably no musician I saw on my whole trip who gave as much pleasure to his audience as Howard Beaumont. I saw an empty deckchair and sat down. 'You've got a good memory,' I said to the woman next to me who knew all the words.

'I can't remember what I had for lunch,' she laughed.

I knew what she meant. I'm sure the last thing I'll forget will be the great archive of Beatles lyrics I have in my head, and there's no better way to beat off the blues than to sing them all out loud.

As I sat there trying to remember what I had for lunch, I could see an attendant striding across the court towards me. Maybe she was going to offer me a blanket.

'Have you got a ticket?'

'No.'

'I'm afraid you can't stay.'

'How much is a ticket?'

'£2.50.'

'All right, I'll have a ticket.'

'The box office is shut.'

'So how can I …?'

'It's shut because the concert finishes in 15 minutes. I'm afraid you can't sit here without a ticket. You'll have to leave.'

I tried to appear outraged while sitting in a deckchair. 'Are you telling me I'm being thrown out of a Howard Beaumont concert?'

She sighed. 'I just work here.'

Now I sighed. We both sighed. Then I did as I was told. But once I was outside, she came and found me and said if I went up onto the veranda I could listen up there. 'Sorry,' she said. 'There are regulars here and they'll complain if someone gets in for nothing.'

A sea mist drifted in and a chill descended. People were in swimming trunks one minute and pullovers the next. They streamed off the beach onto the front where a screaming match was taking place between seagulls, over-tired children and hawkers for the round-the-bay steamer trip. 'Leaving in 10 minutes!' a man wearing a captain's cap shouted in my ear.

I sat on a bench next to a couple eating fish and chips with wooden forks. The gulls were watching them, circling above. I said, 'I should look out for your chips.'

They shuffled closer together. What was I going to do to their chips?

'The gulls,' I said. 'I saw a man in Llandudno lose his ice cream to a gull.'

They still weren't clear what I was driving at.

'The gull will swoop down and have your chips.'

'Scarborough gulls aren't like that,' she said.

I found a place to stay in town. The woman saw my backpack and asked, 'Walking the Cleveland Way?'

'That's right.'

'How far have you come today?'

'From Filey.'

She looked astonished. 'Filey?'

'Yes.' It wasn't far.

'But ... that's the wrong way. You're walking it the wrong way.'

A couple of other hikers had mentioned this, and I couldn't work out what they meant. I was simply walking it south to north, rather than the other way round. What was wrong with that?

I discovered the next day when the wind picked up and I realized the Cleveland Way wasn't really a north-to-south path. It was more northwest to southeast, and I was heading into the prevailing wind. It felt like I was walking uphill, while hikers going the other way whizzed past me as if motorized, calling, 'You're doing it the wrong way.'

'Yes, yes. I know.'

There was a bus called the Seasider, which I could jump on and off all the way up the coast with a day ticket, and so I combined walking with riding. I was in the North York Moors National Park now and finding it difficult to adjust to the large amount of horizon on display. Inland, the heather was trying to bloom on moors that stretched away endlessly, while in the other direction the coastline offered huge beaches with the tide far far out.

This was perfect for the families at Robin Hood's Bay, though, who were all out crabbing in wellies and jellies. The outfits had changed since Turner's time, but the activity still looked the same.

The village, with its red roofs and honey-coloured stone, clung on to the crumbling cliff. This whole stretch of coast suffered badly from erosion, and there were information boards on the path explaining wave attack and reflection – I became familiar with coastal morphodynamics. The consequence for Robin Hood's Bay was 50-foot-high sea walls, making the village look as though it was expecting a siege.

Any connection the eponymous hero had with the village was tenuous at best. 'Robin Hood might have come here once, but not for definite' was about as far as the guidebooks could legally go.

A little further up the coast, Whitby's link with Captain Cook was more genuine, in so far as the young Cook had actually lived there while he was serving his merchant navy apprenticeship. He gave the town something they could market, although work needed to be done to improve his brand. 'I want to see Thomas Cook's house?' said a woman with a serpent tattooed on her neck.

What was really needed was a Hollywood biopic: 'Brad Pitt is Captain James Cook'. Only then would he stand a chance of joining Whitby's A-list celebrity, Dracula, whose status had benefited hugely from movie adaptations.

Dracula, of course, wasn't a local – Transylvania has that sewn up – but Bram Stoker did stay at the Royal Hotel while he was writing the novel, and is reported to have done his research in Whitby library and to have wandered round St Mary's churchyard for inspiration. In fact, Dracula first lands in England at Whitby when his ship is beached here en route for London. He comes ashore disguised as a dog and sinks his teeth into the townsfolk.

The result is a thriving little industry: there's an annual goth weekend; a Halloween night that gets bigger each year; and I can report that the Dracula Experience on the harbour front is doing much better business than Captain Cook's museum.

Of all the coastal towns and villages along the Cleveland Way, however, the one that was most attractive was the one that shouted the least loudly. Staithes, built round a stream that had punched its way through the sandstone cliffs, is a rare and unspoilt discovery, saved by its lack of vehicular access.

There is a minor link to Captain Cook here – he worked for a greengrocer on the harbour front before he heard the call of the sea; maybe it was where he heard the call of the sea – but there's no fuss made. This is just a sleepy ex-fishing village, as pretty as a doll's house and in places as fragile. In the 19th century an artists' colony grew up here, the Northern Impressionists, and, apart from better plumbing, Staithes can't have changed much since. I crept round the tiny alleyways, the cottages tightly packed and built at all angles. They were all different, although they had one factor in common: a *To Let* sign outside, holiday homes by the dozen.

In Staithes I came across a fish factory where a woman told me if I ever wanted fresh fish, to phone and she'd tell me what the catch was that day. She'd pack what I wanted in an ice box and it would be with me by the morning. I was so impressed I bought one of her smoked mackerel for a pound. I'd felt starved of good food like this and I went down to the harbour and sat licking my oily fish slowly and luxuriously as if it were an ice cream. There were a number of families on the quay, but I noticed I had a whole bench to myself.

At Loftus I took to the cliff path again. I needed to ask directions from the main road, but before I could say anything, a local approached me and said, 'Walking the Cleveland Way?' The first Geordie accent I'd heard.

'That's right.'

'The path to Whitby?'

'Saltburn.'

'Saltburn, but that's …'

'I know. I'm walking it the wrong way.'

He looked at me very strangely. What sort of weird person was I? He directed me back to the path through Skinningrove. 'Don't get mugged on the way down.'

I laughed, but he was serious. Unlike everywhere else on this coast, Skinningrove had gone to great lengths to make itself unappealing to the visitor. Terraced housing went right down to the beachfront where normally there would have been bucket and spade shops and shellfish stalls.

Instead of a harbour and a promenade there were some lumps of concrete, a couple of tractors to haul boats up on the shingle, and some sheds that looked as though they'd been repaired with bits from the other sheds that now had holes in themselves.

I never felt I was going to be mugged, but that was because I saw no one, just some mangy cats squabbling. The only sound was an old Queen song being blasted out from an upstairs window.

The coast path soon led me back to more lonely places. The wind had picked up. The late afternoon sun shone fiercely and everything was crispy dry. The cliffs rose to great heights here, sheer and terrifying. I came to one cliff-face that had been turned into Kittiwake City for the nesting season. Every ledge, no matter how cramped, had been turned into accommodation, and the bird traffic to and from was so heavy you wondered how they didn't collide with each other or at least knock the occasional nest off. Their shrill cry was supposed to say, 'Kittiwake, kittiwake,' but I couldn't make that out at all. They were saying, 'Pound of carrots, pound of carrots,' but that was no name for a seabird.

Then, over a headland, out of the coastal plain sprung Teesside, the sun glinting on a skyline of refineries and cooling towers, with big tankers and container ships queuing offshore to enter the docks. The conurbations of the Northeast lay from here on up. It felt as though one road was ending, and another very different one beginning.

I played two open mics on the Cleveland Way, and they continued the trend of one bad night, one good. In Scarborough I turned up at the Castle Tavern where a crowd of lads, straight from football training, filled the room. A brief assessment of the situation told me they hadn't come to listen to a ukulele player, or any other sort of musician for that matter. The teenager organizing the evening was keen to get things going, but I suggested we wait until the footballers quietened down.

'We'll soon sort them out,' he said, and he got on the stage and played very loudly, which certainly did sort them out: they all drank up and left. The trouble was that without the footballers the bar was almost empty. I was used to this sort of situation and it didn't bother me any more, but I felt sorry for the young host. Open mics were a good little earner for a teenager, and he needed to convince the management he was worth it. 'It's normally really busy,' he said to me, and I wondered how many times I'd heard that over the past month.

A couple of his friends turned up and played, but he was still short of an audience. There was just one drinker at the bar. He pointed his finger and said to me, 'I can't stand it when they play other people's songs. I mean, what's the point? Anyone can do that. I'd do my own stuff. My music.'

'What do you play?'

'I don't play anything. But if I did, I mean.'

I didn't dare disagree with him. Instead I got up and played three songs, all of which were covers. Afterwards he came up to me again and I thought he was going tell me I was a disgrace, but he said, 'Very good.'

'Thank you.'

'I mean it's not easy being left-handed, is it?'

'You get used to it.'

'No, no. I'm left-handed. I know. It's a right-handed person's world.'

'To a point.'

'It makes you tough, though. I was bullied at school for being left-handed.'

I doubted that was the reason he was bullied.

'I was made to write with my right hand. It screwed me up. I've never had a management job. It's all different now of course. Left-handed kids have it easy. They have their own left-handed pencil sharpeners and stuff. Napoleon was left-handed, you know?'

'Was he?'

'So was Buzz Aldrin.'

I went and bought a pasta salad on special offer from Tesco Express and had an early night.

Saltburn, the following night, couldn't have been more different. But then the town itself was a place apart. It was another of these planned resorts, an old fishing hamlet that had fallen under the gaze of a Victorian entrepreneur keen to provide somewhere for the local working classes – Teessiders in this case – to spend their money. Hotels sprung up, then a promenade, and no seaside town was worth visiting unless it had a pier. Streets were laid out and named after gemstones: Ruby Street, Emerald, Amber; a funicular railway ascended the cliff. The new town was completed at the end of the 19th century. By the start of the 20th it was already in decline.

It's a familiar story, but whereas other resorts had reinvented themselves as conference centres or ferry ports, Saltburn was left just the way it was. It appeared locked in its own Groundhog Day, stalled at the end of the Victorian era.

There was little deference to tourism, but that was because no one in their right mind would come here for a beach holiday, certainly not the folk from Teesside. You got the feeling little happened here; nothing changed. The North Sea was always the same shade of grey, and every Friday night the locals went along to SOAP, the Saltburn Open Acoustic Platform.

For an open mic to have its own acronym suggested it was a well-respected event rather than just some pub trying to get customers in on a quiet night. Indeed, SOAP had been going so long it was a community fixture. It wasn't even held in a pub; it was in the local Conservative Club, and if all Con Clubs are like Saltburn's I might check my local one out.

Martin was the host. When I asked him if I could play, he glanced doubtfully at his long list. But then said, 'Have you been here before?'

'No. Just here for the night.'

'On business, eh? We'll fit you in.'

There was a generosity of spirit about Saltburn that was infectious. It was rare to find an event like this that appealed to all ages, but there were teenagers as well as pensioners here, and everyone was keen to join in.

A 16-year-old took the stage and sang 'The Boxer', and the whole room sang 'Li Li Li'. A man about the same age as Paul McCartney played 'All My Loving' on the keyboard and everyone knew the song by heart. 'Completely self-taught,' he said to me proudly afterwards. 'Never had a lesson. No one here has.'

Everyone looked slightly sunburnt, as if the good

weather had caught them unawares.

'It doesn't shine often round here,' said a man with a red neck.

'You have to make the most of it,' said his wife. 'We've been sitting in Derek's garden all afternoon.'

These were people who had known each other for years, been coming here for years. They were proud of what they had, and they assumed I had come especially. 'Where are you from?' a woman asked me.

'Derbyshire.'

'That's nothing! We had someone from Australia last week.'

There was nothing makeshift about SOAP. It started promptly; there was good equipment and there was an interval. It was a Friday night ritual, a signal for the end of the working week. If you had work, that was. The industrial skyline of Teesside that I had seen from the cliff path was, I was informed, redundant, and unemployment rising. 'The steel mills were closed down long ago,' said a man in his thirties, shaking his head.

'What do people do for work round here now then?'

'Not a lot. Some people write songs about it.'

My turn to play came and Martin announced me. 'We've got a travelling salesman next. First time ever at Saltburn Acoustic. Ladies and Gentlemen ...'

The open mic ended at 11pm, but they carried on with a jam until the early hours.

Everyone involved with SOAP was doing it for the love of it, and you could feel the positive effect it had. Coming into a town on a coast path in minstrel mode I knew I had a romanticized view of things, but in Saltburn I began to wonder whether a regular open-mic session might just be able to contribute to world peace and harmony. Disaffected youths the world over might behave differently if they had an open mic in their neighbourhood. Inner city strife cured overnight. Doctors would prescribe an open mic to people with depression. Lottery-funded grants would be awarded for equipment. Westminster could have one every Wednesday night, so as not to clash with the one on a Tuesday at the UN. The message would be clear: don't bottle up that stress; don't take an automatic weapon into your supermarket to release tension; get yourself down to an open mic. Tonight!

Before I left SOAP I met Steve who said to me, 'I film all these you know. I'll put you on YouTube.'

The following morning I took my place among the dog-walkers, joggers and pony-riders and set out for Redcar along Saltburn beach, a vast expanse of sand so flat that Malcolm Campbell came here in 1922 and attempted to break the land-speed record in *Bluebird*.

All I could associate Redcar with was the race track. 'The 2.30 from Redcar' was the only time I'd heard the town mentioned. It was visible in the distance and I thought it would take half an hour to reach it, but it was like a mirage and seemed to get further away. It didn't matter. I was walking with a spring in my step. I was up there on YouTube with the best of them.

From Redcar it was a simple bus ride to Middlesbrough along the A66. I hadn't planned to travel this route, and it was a real thrill when I saw the road sign. I tried to savour every detail: the huge container yards, the train chugging by, the burger restaurant, the woman in front of me explaining to her five-year-old how hot the sun is ('very very hot'). You get your kicks, on the A66.

When I got to Newcastle I went straight to the Sage, the splendid concert hall complex in Gateshead on the south bank of the Tyne. I asked the assistant in the box office what was on that night. He said, 'Nothing.'

'This is the Sage?'

'That's right.'

'Gateshead's "international home for music and musical discovery"?'

'That's right.'

'And there's nothing on tonight?'

'No.'

'A Saturday night?'

'No.'

So I went to the tourist office across the Tyne at the Central Arcade to see what concerts were on around town and they said, 'Ask in the Sage.'

I ended up flicking through the 'what's on' page in the local newspaper, while listening to an American couple asking the best way to get to Edinburgh and trying to understand the assistant's Geordie accent. 'Excuse me?' was their response to everything she said.

I was aware I could hear 'Danny Boy' over the sound system. Initially, I thought it was just muzak, but the singer had a lovely voice. It was so enchanting I was about to ask at the desk if they knew who it was when I realized that it wasn't coming over the sound system at all. The nearer I got to the side door, the louder it became.

I went out and found myself in a beautiful Edwardian arcade with a mosaic floor and walls decorated with tiles in brown, green and purple hues, peacock colours. And standing against one wall was a young woman with her arms behind her back, head up, singing 'Danny Boy'.

She hit every note perfectly, and with the ceramic acoustics of the arcade, her voice echoed off the walls and came at you from all directions. It was impossible to walk by her without stopping to listen.

She had a semi-circle of people before her and they were transfixed. A box for donations was at her feet, overflowing with coins. Even the hardest-nosed passer-by was charmed and put something in. Had she walked away still singing, we would have followed her like the Pied Piper.

Newcastle was a lively and striking city, full of surprises and full of character. But whenever I think back to my visit, the first thing I see is that girl standing in the Central Arcade like Mother Bereft, singing 'Danny Boy' with a passion that made you believe it was her own dear child about to sail away forever, and that he would be able to hear her voice all the way across the ocean.

I had friends in Newcastle. They told me there an open mic down at the Free Trade Inn that night. There wasn't, but there was a fabulous sunset, looking straight down the

Tyne through five elegant bridges.

The barmaid told me to try the Cumberland Arms. There wasn't an open mic up there either. 'Thursday,' the barman said.

'That's open-mic night?'

'No, that's Wednesday. Thursday is ukulele night.'

At last, the respect the ukulele deserved. My little uke had taken a lot of flak on the way up the country – 'It's a bonsai guitar, look' – but here in Newcastle it had its own night. What other instrument could say that?

I was told to try the Tyne Bar, not too far away. There wasn't an open mic there either, but I did meet a party of women out on the start of a pub crawl.

'What's that in your bag?'

'Ukulele.'

'I love a ukulele.'

They all loved a ukulele. Newcastle was ukulele heaven.

'Play us a tune,' one of them asked.

'What, here?' We were sitting under railway arches. It was perfect.

'Yeah.'

'Now?'

'Now! It's her birthday,' she said, putting her arm over one of her friends.

At last! An opportunity to play 'Happy Birthday'. I played it with gusto and they all sang like a rugby team.

'What else do you know?'

And we were off. Who needed an open mic? I played and they sang. They shouted requests, and I played something else.

'Can you play "I Will Survive"?'

'Sure.'

I couldn't, but it didn't matter. They sang what they wanted anyway.

I walked with them down to the city centre past the Millennium Bridge with its beautiful double blade of an arch. They all stopped to take photos as the lights changed colour and the bridge looked as graceful as a butterfly. I realized then that they weren't from Newcastle; they were out-of-towners.

'There's nothing like this in Darlington,' they said. 'Saturday night in Newcastle is like a carnival.'

It was. It seemed as though all the women in the North-east were out on hen nights. High heels, long legs, fancy dress. A group dressed as sailors paraded down towards the river, screaming and giggling. Men stood outside the pubs, leering. A woman stumbled and yelped as her heel broke. She took her shoe off and showed it to the men.

'They cost £120,' she cried.

'Bit of superglue, won't know the difference.'

'They cost £120!'

'Come and have a drink.'

The women happily went into the pub with the men. I thought back to the street pastors in Worthing who carried flip-flops round with them for broken heel situations just like this. Where were they when you needed them?

The night was warm and full of energy. A comedy club was hauling people off the streets. 'He's doing his Edinburgh show. See it now!' A minibus pulled up and out rolled another hen party, all of them dressed as Superwoman.

A firework went off and some gulls took off in fright. I watched them fly up and then settle in the eaves of the Tyne Bridge. I was amazed to spot a colony of kittiwakes up there, as tightly packed as they had been on the cliff path. The bridge was lit up so that it looked like a cruise ship in the water, but the gulls had found the dark recesses, and they snuggled in there, ignoring the parade of flesh below, trying to get an early night.

Sunday was official hangover day in Newcastle. Everyone spoke in a whisper. You hid behind a newspaper. If you went outside, you wore sunglasses.

I sat in a café courtyard on another sunny morning and ordered a bowl of porridge.

'Porridge?' The waiter looked at me as if I was foreign or a drunk who hadn't made it home yet. I wanted to tell him how hard it had been for me to eat a reasonable diet on this trip; how I had grown to hate the words 'full' and 'English' before the word 'breakfast'; how I never felt like eating before a performance and afterwards everywhere but the Indians and Chinese had shut; how gloomy sitting in a restaurant on my own made me feel; and how I wasn't going to eat fast food no matter how hungry I was. So I ended up in supermarkets, eating sandwiches, which was why I was so delighted to see porridge on his menu.

'Yes porridge,' I said. 'Unless you've got a kipper.'

I went down to the quayside where there was a Sunday market and a large area that had been covered with sand to create a beach. Kids built sandcastles and adults sat in deckchairs in the middle of the city. It was the kind of bizarre installation that won the Turner Prize.

Almost as bizarre as the Robert Breer floats in the Baltic gallery across the river. These were abstract shapes, some the size of a wall, others in the form of a dropped blanket, but all mechanized so they moved imperceptibly around the room. You could sit there for hours waiting to see what happened if they collided. It was still-life in slow motion, which just about summed up Newcastle on a Sunday.

The only place I could find to play was in Tynemouth – Newcastle-on-sea – at the end of the Metro line. I thought it would be a backwater and the open mic would be a rundown Sunday evening affair. But I was very wrong. The Priory was a pub as big as a barn, and heaving after a sunny afternoon. The clientele had recovered from their Saturday night and were dressed to display their tans. It was another pick-up joint, and so noisy, an open mic had no business being held there at all.

A corner of the room had been roped off, and there was an amp and microphone at the ready and a guitar on its stand. But no sign of anyone hosting. I squeezed my way to the bar and asked. They said Jonny was around somewhere.

I sat in an armchair and waited. A man with a bee earring noticed my ukulele. He nodded and said, 'You playing?'

I said I was, and he looked around at the packed room. 'It's not going to be easy.'

'No.'

'I've played in places like this; it's hard work.'

'So what do you do?'

He shrugged. 'You got to win them over.'

I wondered what he was trying to say. My way of dealing with places like this was to play my three songs fast and get out faster.

'You have to bare a bit of your soul,' he said. 'You have to show them something they've never seen before.'

I didn't like the sound of that.

'Good luck,' he said, and turned back to his girlfriend.

Jonny turned up. He said, 'I was worrying no one else was going to show.'

I was feeling unmotivated. I said, 'I don't think this lot will appreciate any ukulele music.'

'Course they will. Give it a go. You get a free drink. What have you got to lose? I'll go first.'

He played a string of chart hits. Afterwards he said to me, 'Sound system is crap. Rubbish. Don't know what they've done to it. Your turn.'

It was like singing to a wall. The only reaction I got was from people who turned their backs. For the first time I sensed they were feeling sorry for me. 'What is that 58-year-old doing standing there playing his silly little guitar, singing songs from 1950 and wearing trousers with zips round the knees?'

I didn't know what to do. The man with the earring had told me to bare my soul, but if I bared anything to this lot they'd point and laugh at the size. I had no idea how to bare my soul anyway. What was I going to do? Wander from table to table like a lap dancer?

I stood there, playing on automatic pilot, looking over their heads, trying to spot the end of the song on the horizon, and feeling feeble because the truth was beginning to dawn. It was easy to play to an audience that was clapping along with you, but a crowd like this needed to be tackled and turned around. That was what the man had meant: the true performer believed there was no audience he couldn't win over. My trouble was I was more than happy to accept defeat.

'Sounded great,' said Jonny afterwards. He gave me his flyer, a list of songs he performed. 'I play my own stuff as well,' and he showed me his CD. 'But I have to play covers here, it's part of the deal.'

He was trying to make a living at it: playing solo gigs, playing in bands, hosting open mics. He had his Myspace and Facebook pages and YouTube videos promoting his album; and there was such a good music scene in Newcastle he could play any night he wanted. 'You have to play live, it's the future.'

But it was tough. No one wanted to pay for music these days. All these musicians dreamed of 'making it' but no one was really sure what that meant any more. Was it winning *X Factor*? Or was it gigging round Newcastle playing your own music? It would be awful to make it and not realize it.

'You need a certain amount of talent,' said Jonny, 'but right place, right time is what's important.'

So is baring the soul, I wanted to say.

'Have you had your free beer?' he asked.

You didn't often get a free beer at open mics, and this

didn't seem like the sort of place to be so generous. I pushed my way to the bar again and told a barman I was owed a beer.

He laughed. 'Why?'

'I just played the open mic.'

'What, that mandolin?'

'Ukulele.'

'You were awful.'

'Thanks.'

I didn't mind. I could take constructive criticism like 'You were awful'. And anyway, nothing could spoil my fondness for Newcastle. It was the kind of city you came to for a weekend and ended up staying for years. It was honest and unfussy, full of artists and musicians, and, apart from the odd barman, people seemed to want to help and encourage one another all the time.

On my last night I was invited to a party given by the writer Peter Mortimer, who ran the poetry publisher Iron Press. He lived in Cullercoats in the only lilac-painted house in the street. The guests were poets and friends of poets and they took it in turns to perform a variety show in the yard.

A magician, a cellist, a couple of cabaret performers: an open mic in a backyard on a warm August evening. I wasn't naive enough to believe that every night in Newcastle was like this, but I suspected there was always the potential.

I was asked to play my ukulele, and afterwards people said nice things. When I told them I was heading to Edinburgh, they just assumed I was going to play at the festival. I played the innocent, but they said, 'You'll go down great up there.'

It was dangerous to start believing this sort of thing, because I had no idea how to impress myself upon the festival in any way. But there seemed no escape from it now. Edinburgh was on road signs, straight up the A1. I was being drawn towards it.

I was back at the piano with Jools Holland, saying, 'Well Jools, I suppose it was Edinburgh that changed everything.'

chapter eleven

caledonia dreamin'

Try telling the residents of Alnwick in Northumberland that Edinburgh is the only festival to be seen at in August, and they'll politely inform you otherwise: you're clearly unaware of the International Music Festival that visits their town every summer.

I was certainly unaware of it. I just bumped right into it as I changed buses. One minute I was heading up to Berwick-upon-Tweed, the next I had a crowd of Polish dancers in my face accompanied by a brass band in national costume.

The band had a regimental air. The dancers had fierce smiles. Their choreography said, 'This is how we do it in Poland. It's how we've always done it, and it's how we'll do it for ever more.'

The Poles were followed by Romanians who were Tiller Girls by comparison. Then came a troop from Brittany who danced with their noses in the air. Finally, a Northumbrian folk trio took to the stage, proving that when it came to colourful costumes, nothing made a splash quite like grey and brown terylene.

There was a lot of slapping of thighs and stick banging in Alnwick that day, and while the festival wasn't perhaps as risqué as some shows in Edinburgh, like Puppetry of the Penis, there was a party spirit. Only the weather refused to co-operate. Dark clouds flew over the market square like helicopters fighting a forest fire, dumping gallons of water on the crowd below. There was a tarpaulin over the stage but not the audience, and we would scatter with such speed when the rain came that the band who had travelled all the way across Europe to be here could easily have taken it personally.

The mayor was acting as MC. 'It's only a shower,' he said, from under the canvas. Ann, his assistant, was the real star of the show. She was busy selling raffle tickets one minute and mopping up the stage the next. A thankless job. As soon as she finished, it started to rain again. The mayor announced they were opening the town hall for the aeolian harp recital. Everyone rushed inside, partly to hear the harp, mostly for the chance to shelter.

The harpist looked serene sitting beneath a picture of the Queen and surrounded by cardboard boxes. She played and sang the Burns song, 'My Love Is Like A Red, Red, Rose'. Then she announced, 'I'd like to play "Mountains of Mourne", which I'm going to dedicate to my mother,' and she looked over to me, lovingly. In fact, she was looking at her mother who was sitting at my side, but it was an unsettling moment.

After another song, Ann came in and informed us the stage was almost dry and 'The French are going to risk it.' The audience had to quickly choose between another harp tune or the chance of seeing French people fall over. It was a no-brainer. Everyone hurried outside.

There were musicians and dancers from all over the world in Alnwick and there was a camaraderie that only showed cracks when it came to merchandizing. The different groups had tables around the market square where they sold their indigenous arts and crafts and here the competition was strong. They all sold CDs, but the Romanians offered bags and purses and Dracula Castle snow scenes as well. They were easily out-sold, though, by the Indian team from Gujarat who offered a range of jewellery, slippers, leather goods and Taj Mahal pencil and rubber sets. The Brits, of course, were nowhere in this league. On a table by himself, I found Northumbrian folk singer Andrew Lobb, who just had his CD for sale. I felt like telling him: Andrew, you're never going to get anywhere in the music business until you get some Cheviot sheep fridge magnets, mate. At least he was being more industrious than the French who were clearly above fund-raising and didn't even have a stall.

The day was lost to the weather. The music stopped and would restart in the evening. I had wanted to walk some of the way up the Northumberland coast, but with the mist down, all views were lost, so I took the bus again, and sat among families in anoraks, trying to amuse themselves. At Seahouses there was a trip out to the Farne Islands on offer, but it was hard to get excited by the idea of visiting somewhere just offshore that you couldn't even see. The gaunt Bamburgh Castle was only slightly more promising, looming out of the sea mist like a prison. 'Look, Grace Darling's buried over there,' said a passenger and even the driver looked across into Bamburgh churchyard.

In the evening I got as far as Berwick, which was a grey town anyway, and in the mist appeared to have lost all shape. The town walls, the roads, the sky, the River Tweed itself, they were all the colour of an old saucepan.

I found a place to stay and walked into town around the walls. An elderly man was walking his elderly dog. 'He's 12 years old,' he said. 'I don't think he knows why we come out here any more.'

It was a sad situation: the dog who couldn't remember why his master had to go walking on the walls twice a day.

The little dog had a little dump. He had a look that said: I might as well, since we're out here. The man looked at me and said, 'I haven't got a bag.'

'I've got one,' I said. But he wasn't interested.

I'd been told to try the Pilot Inn for an open mic, but when I got there it was the wrong night. 'Tuesday,' said the barman. 'It's only once a month anyway.'

'No. It's every week now,' said his only customer.

'It's every month.'

'It's every week.'

I wanted to say, 'It doesn't really matter because today's Monday.'

'What do you play?' said the customer.

'Ukulele.'

'Not another one.'

I walked round the town, which by now was so misty it was like a Sherlock Holmes movie. Lights shone out of the gloom ahead: the welcoming glow of the Magna Tandoori.

I sat on my own in this big, red restaurant. Every

noise I made echoed round the room: the crunch of my poppadom; the spoon on the metallic pickle tray. Only the waiter made no sound. He would appear from nowhere at my shoulder and whisper, 'Spinach biriani, sir.'

'Arrgh!'

Eventually more diners came in. One man threw his car keys down on the table and said to his wife, 'You're driving home.'

They ordered a ridiculous amount of food. The waiter had to join two tables together. The woman said, 'What's this going to cost?'

'The money doesn't matter!'

She muttered something back.

'What?'

'I just said it's a lot of food.'

'Life's for enjoying. You worry too much.'

'Michael!' she hissed.

'Don't Michael me.'

He got upset about his rice and was rude to the waiter. He drank too much and was rude to another waiter. He was a genuinely unattractive man. There were six other people in the room and every one of us felt sorry for his wife.

The following day I slipped across the border into Scotland. There was no fuss. I saw no banners or road signs, just a man in a tracksuit climbing on board the bus and speaking in a strong Scottish accent to the driver. 'Where's Joe?'

'No on today.'

'I thought Joe was on.'

'No today.'

He looked stumped. He stood there a moment then said, 'I'll no bother then,' and stepped down.

My plan was to take a circuitous route to Edinburgh, via Glasgow and Stirling, an open mic in each, and then hit the festival primed. I felt confident. My playing had improved beyond recognition. I had a range of material now – and not just rhythm and blues; I'd learnt a couple of Neil Innes songs, some Hank Williams, a Cole Porter. I had some chat for each number as well, and I could even exchange techno-speak with the mixing desk. 'You've got to take the top off; the ukulele doesn't like much gain.'

I was super fit from all the walking. I was living a healthy life for a rock 'n' roll tourist. My only brush with drugs this trip had been some anti-inflammatories for a pulled back – a nice mellow high. I was in good condition. So why were people looking at me oddly in the street? Why in Newcastle had that leafleter on the quayside not bothered with me? And why was this woman in Glasgow offering me a sandwich? 'It's sausage and egg,' she said and waved it at me.

'Thanks. I'm not hungry.'

'There's nothing wrong with it. There were two in the packet. I only wanted one.'

When I went into a shopping arcade to use the toilet, I noticed a security guard watching me. But instead of throwing me out, he put his hand on my shoulder and asked if I was lost.

'I'm not lost.'

'There are places to sit down if you want.'

'I'm fine, thanks.'

I went to the gents and looked at myself in the mirror. As I feared, the old homeless face was back: matted grey beard, weather-beaten head, bags under eyes from sleeping on the bus. How could I feel so good and look so bad? I smelt my shirt. I needed to throw everything into a laundrette and crawl in after it.

Scotland didn't feel like a foreign place the way Wales had; there were no signs in two languages – not this far south anyway. Glasgow did feel alien, but simply because it was so big. It was the opposite sort of city experience to Newcastle. I'd heard on the radio that it was the 'murder capital of Europe', as if assault was a local tradition. Maybe that was what all the foreign tourists were doing here, walking round with cameras at the ready, waiting to witness a shooting.

I followed an Italian party on a walking tour. They wore yellow disposable rain jackets that were really just dustbin liners with arm holes, the word 'Scotland' written on the front, a thistle on the back. They looked like sunny people in a rainy city.

They were led round the Italian Centre, and then to the Gallery of Modern Art, where they took pictures of the statue of Wellington with a traffic cone on his head. The guide pouted and gesticulated. I couldn't understand what she was saying, but I think that made the buildings sound more interesting than they probably were.

In George Square they climbed back on their Viaggi bus and went back to their hotel for dinner. Leaving me alone with my couscous salad in a plastic tub.

At one time Glasgow was a notoriously difficult place for English acts to play. Comedy careers never recovered from a mauling at theatres like the Glasgow Empire. Des O'Connor once fell to the floor in a fake faint his routine was going so badly. Rock bands from south of the border found it dangerous enough to ask for more money.

These days the power has shifted to the performer – certainly on the open-mic circuit anyway. There were more opportunities in Glasgow than anywhere I'd visited, more places to play than it seemed could possibly be sustained. In one block between Sauchiehall and Bath Street, I counted four bars advertising *open mic tonight*. And there were more up towards the West End. If you didn't like the look of one audience, you just went on to the next.

The first place I looked in brought back memories of the heavy metal evening in Llandudno, so I passed on that one. Another was a student bar and had the stage right in the window so performers looked as though they were in the Red Light District of Amsterdam. I walked on until I came across the oddly named the Butterfly and the Pig, and when I peered down from street level into the basement window I saw two guitarists on the stage, sitting down and playing together in an easy manner. They were pleasingly middle-aged, and there were comfy couches and armchairs in the bar. It looked more like a gentleman's club than a music venue.

It was the right choice. The evening was one of the highlights of the whole tour. Nothing to do with me, I should add. Mine was a forgettable performance where, unforgivably, I played with an out-of-tune ukulele. It was clear from the start my C string was flat, but whenever I attempted to re-tune, I just made it worse. I considered doing a Des O'Connor, but in the end tried to avoid the C altogether. It's barely enough playing an instrument with four strings; reducing that to three can sound a little thin.

It was the two guitarists I had seen from the street who made the evening so memorable. From outside they had looked like two blokes just belting it out, but the minute I walked in I could tell these were the best two musicians I'd heard since Brighton. They were playing swing guitar, gypsy jazz. Tam played rhythm and Tom played the solos. Energetic stuff, well executed, and the audience wanted them to play all night. There were a few other players, like the man who announced he was going to play a song written by someone who used to live up the road, namely Donovan, and proceeded to play a perfectly good version of 'Catch The Wind', but if a speaker had fallen on him halfway through and put him out of action, there would have been no complaints if it meant Tam and Tom came back sooner.

The only other performance of note that night came from a pushy mum, who arrived with her teenage son. He sat nervously clutching his guitar, while she fussed over him and told him to pull his trousers up. She looked at me and said, 'They wear them so low. I don't know how they don't fall down.'

When his turn came, she ushered him up there. 'Go on!' And then proceeded to talk to her neighbour throughout his whole performance. 'He plays all the time at home, sitting in his bedroom. I reckon he's better than half of those on *Britain's Got Talent*. He writes his own songs too. I keep telling him to make a CD. If you can play a musical instrument you'll never be short of a bob or two, that's what my father always said.'

The boy was very tense. He forgot his words, and looked at his guitar all the time ('I told him to look at the audience').

The small crowd understood his burden and gave him a supportive cheer at the end. 'You didn't say you wrote the songs yourself,' she said as he sat back down, pale and shaky.

Tam and Tom came back for one last set. They played everything you wanted to hear from the Django Reinhardt Hot Club era: 'Coquette', 'Exactly Like You', 'I Saw Stars'. They really *were* better than anything you saw on *Britain's Got Talent*.

Two women with a bottle of Asti Spumante sat next to me. They saw my ukulele and one said, 'Are you going to play that thing or what?'

'I'm afraid you missed me.'

'Thank Christ for that,' said her friend.

Ah, audience from the old school. It didn't matter. They couldn't hurt me. I had come to Glasgow to pump myself up, and, although I'd played badly – a mere technical issue – Tom and Tam had shown me that all I needed was a bit more musicianship and flair, a little more of a relaxed manner, a larger repertoire, and a bit more experience. And I'd be …

I walked passed the Slouch club on the way back – the bar with the stage in the window. It wasn't a students' bar at all. A man in his forties was up there singing 'Mr Tambourine Man', sounding as though he needed to blow his nose.

I listened to him for a minute and fell back to earth like a bag of logs. Just watching him from behind, singing as if he was delivering a speech to shareholders, made me realize I would always have much more in common with him than I ever would with Tom and Tam.

Stage presence was an area I knew I needed to work on. Tom and Tam really looked like they were enjoying themselves. Their shoulders rolled in rhythm, their feet tapped in time. Their eyebrows were animated.

This sort of thing didn't come easily to me. In the Elderly Brothers I was the frontman because I was the singer, and I imagined that simply by taking on that role I would automatically strut about a bit. It was only when someone was mean enough to make a video of us that we realized how unlike a band we looked. Our drummer kept dropping his sticks. Our bass player was concentrating so hard you could see his lips move as he counted 12 bars. Our lead guitarist, despite wearing a headband and sunglasses, still couldn't hide the fact he worked in IT. Our keyboard player jumped up and down like a Thunderbird puppet. I, meanwhile, stood at the front, all but motionless.

I pointed out to the others that if you looked closely you could see my left foot rise and fall two inches every two beats. They weren't impressed. They reminded me that Ozzy Osbourne had gone so far as biting the head off a bat live on stage to fulfil his frontman's role, and that I needed to put more effort in.

After much thought and experimentation I decided to play to my strengths ... and not move at all. I cut out even the tapping left foot. I would stand still for the entire set. I even gave myself a sobriquet: the Plank.

In a band you can get away with such eccentricities. On your own you just look like an idiot. So the next morning in Glasgow I stood in front of the mirror with my ukulele round my neck and practised a few movements. I swung my shoulders from side to side – it looked oddly unco-ordinated. I rocked the ukulele up and down in time – it looked like I was paddling a canoe. I leant forward and tried to give myself a face full of urgency – I looked like I should be sectioned.

In the end, I choreographed a side-stepping movement combined with a rhythmic nod of the head, which was better than standing there like a cardboard cutout, but only just.

I left Glasgow without witnessing one murder. I couldn't wait any longer. I was keen to spend the day in Stirling, a city which could match Glasgow's bloodshed rate, but only if you got historical.

The infamous Battle of Stirling Bridge in 1297 had a body count of over 5,000, which is a shocking figure, even if it was a battle between the English and Scottish. William Wallace was the Scottish protagonist and not the sort to take prisoners. History has it that he flayed the body of his adversary Hugh de Cressingham, and took a broad strip of skin from head to foot to make a belt for his sword.

Seventeen years later there was a re-match, this time between Robert the Bruce and Edward II at the Battle of Bannockburn, a village just south of Stirling. Edward wanted to rout the Scottish army and brought in 16,000 men to do the job. It didn't work out the way he planned – fixtures against the Scots rarely do – and Edward left for home a beaten man, with Stirling Castle in the hands of the Scots and 11,000 dead along the banks of the River Forth.

It's hard to imagine any positive legacy coming from these bloody battles, and yet there is an invaluable one: Stirling's enviable tourism pedigree. Not only is there a grand castle and a dramatic history, William Wallace's story has given the city that all-important Hollywood connection, thanks to the Oscar-winning *Braveheart*. There's a priapic monument to the man – Wallace, not Mel Gibson – rising out of the trees on a hill to the north, framed by mountains. Small thanks to a national hero who saved Stirling once, some 800 years ago and now saves it every day.

The Stirling visitor trail doesn't stop there. There's also a link to the *Titanic*. According to a plaque on King Street, engineer William Moyes, born in Stirling, went down with the ship in 1912.

I walked round the town, thinking: this is very promising; Stirling is ticking all the boxes; all it needs now is a Beatles link for a full house.

Surely The Beatles must have played here. They toured

everywhere in the early days. A bit of research quickly told me they hadn't played in Stirling itself, but they had in Bridge of Allan, a couple of miles out of town. And it wasn't just any concert. This was in 1963 and they were booed off stage.

A January Saturday night. The incipient Fab Four had just returned from Hamburg and were on a short four-concert tour of Scotland, billed as *The Love Me Do Boys*. They played at Museum Hall in Bridge of Allan for a £40 fee. But the audience was small and made up of drunk farmers who had come into town hoping to meet women. Instead, they got four young lads from Liverpool playing them three hours of rhythm and blues.

The evening degenerated into a punch-up. Coins were thrown at the group. They were jeered and sent packing to Dingwall, their next concert. Recalling the night, the booking agent said he didn't take much on the door, but did find three shillings in change on the stage afterwards.

Museum Hall fell into disrepair and closed as a venue in the 1970s. Now it's been developed into smart apartments. The Beatles don't even get a plaque on the wall.

That wouldn't bother the diehard Beatles tourist on a pilgrimage, though. This was a genuine link. So here it was. Stirling, with its castle, bloody history, local hero, Hollywood movie, *Titanic* and Beatles connections. The definitive blue chip tourist town.

It was a hot afternoon, and the Church of the Holy Rude on Castle Hill was the perfect place to cool down. I was drawn in by the sound of an organ; a recital was under way by the church's director of music. He played Haydn, Bach and Handel to an appreciative audience. All was going well until someone applauded in the wrong place.

Heads turned to stare at the philistine who really should have been given a service revolver and asked to go outside. Maybe this was why the audience had no member under 50. I defy anyone of any age to resist Bach's 'Ave Maria', but if you wrap it up in an elitist package and apply rules that you then don't explain to the uninitiated, you're going to get the waxworks audience you deserve. Besides, this business of only applauding at the end of a whole piece rather than after movements is a relatively modern one. When Beethoven and his contemporaries played they wanted to know how they were doing and were happy to get applause in between movements, sometimes even during them. When Stravinsky premiered *The Rite of Spring*, the audience let him know how they felt by fighting in the aisles.

No one is suggesting the good folk of the Holy Rude start getting over emotional, but maybe they could lighten up a little. I wondered if anyone in the audience was a young farmer at that Beatles concert almost 50 years ago, throwing coins.

Stirling Castle was closing by the time I reached the gates, but the real excitement of the afternoon was shaping up in the car park: a live broadcast of the TV show *The Great British Weather*.

A large audience of visitors had formed, thrilled to be involved. 'Come on, who wants to be on telly?' the director had called out. 'Me me me me me!' shouted back the crowd. A man got his comb out and arranged his hair over his bald patch.

The director got them to rehearse their cheers and applause. 'I couldn't hear that. Is that the best you can do?' It was an illustration of the power of TV: well-adjusted adults on a day out to Stirling Castle reverting to 12-year-olds as soon as a camera was pointed at them. I wanted to walk away with disdain, but then I noticed weatherman royalty had arrived: Bill Giles, John Kettley and Michael Fish, all gathered together on the stage. I had to stay. Terrorists could strike at the very heart of Britain if they chose to attack now.

The weathermen signed autographs and posed for photos. We were encouraged to applaud them long and hard. It made me wonder how many people I had applauded on my trip so far: more than 25 open mics' worth, plus an organist already that day, and now three men in sports jackets, who were deserving because they read the weather on telly.

'We're going live in seven minutes,' said the director. 'A word of warning: if you're standing next to anyone you shouldn't be with – wink wink – move out of shot now.'

'I'd be so lucky,' someone called out. The director tried to smile, but he was edgy.

The male presenter put his hand on the female presenter's arse, and got a laugh. 'That's institutionalized sexism in the BBC that is,' quipped another wag in the crowd and got an even bigger laugh. The director frowned: did I tell you you could laugh?

When we finally went live it was all a bit frantic. The weathermen went on camera and had to guess where the sunniest place in the country was. We applauded them again for that. The presenters had to put on kilts and have them blown off by a wind machine. Bagpipers marched through the set playing the theme from the Scott's Porage Oats advert – which no one I asked knew the name of – and that was that. All that equipment, all that effort, and now they were packing up. 'Thank you very much,' said the director, 'you've been the best audience we've had.'

'Yeah sure,' said the crowd.

'I mean it, a good afternoon's work.'

A good afternoon's work? Robert the Bruce and William Wallace had watched it all from their stone plinths outside the castle. In the same amount of time it took to set up and make a TV broadcast, they had slaughtered 11,000 people. Now that was an afternoon's work.

I needed a good performance from myself that night. I planned to take the train to Edinburgh after my open mic, and I wanted to arrive on a wave.

The main street in Stirling was busy on a warm evening. Lads had their shirts off, and were shouting football slogans. A police car drove by and a beer can was thrown at it.

In a pub at the bottom of the hill there was some good Scottish music. The bar was packed, although the small band played with little deference to the crowd. This was traditional music. You liked it or you left it.

If you left it you went up to Nicky-Tams, which was where the open mic for the evening was. 'We're just about to start,' said the barman. 'Upstairs.'

I went upstairs, but it was empty.

'Not for long,' said the barman, rearranging chairs. He went back down and pushed up the few locals in the bar 'Do we have to?' said one.

'Yes, you do. And watch your language, we've got a visitor.'

He pushed the barmaid upstairs as well, but that was because she was the only one who knew how to work the equipment. She was also the opening act. She put a guitar round her neck and started to play and sing with a good strong voice. She had downloaded her lyrics onto her phone and strapped it to the mic so she could read from it while playing, something I'd never seen before. It worked well, except there was a slight pause in the song every time she scrolled down a page.

A group of Norwegians who had been up at the TV broadcast came in. They looked ready for a party. There weren't any other people to play yet, but the barmaid said to me, 'We'll do shifts, eh?'

I played my best set. I put everything into it. I added my new stage moves, my shoulder swing and slight hip readjustment every four bars. The Norwegians weren't sure what to make of it, but gave me the benefit of the doubt. All was going well until halfway through the third song it all kicked off in the flat upstairs.

Drills, hammers, plumbing noises. 'He's doing up his bathroom,' said the barman. 'He works on it every night.'

So there I was playing 'Jailhouse Rock' while trying to compete with someone hammering the pipes above my head. I wouldn't have minded if he'd been in time; it might have added a bit of percussion, but the random bursts of electric drill and planing gave my set an experimental dimension that didn't sit well with the ukulele.

The Norwegians weren't bothered. Nor were the Dutch party who'd joined them. They'd all had a few drinks by now and they swayed about as I pressed on with a version of 'I'm The Urban Spaceman' with assorted masonry drills. Even the locals were getting into the spirit. When they went out for a smoke, they asked me to play louder so they could hear it in the street.

The barmaid and I took it in turns for the whole evening. I played everything I knew. Eventually the DIY upstairs stopped and in the sweaty room the audience closed in. They sang along and I could see how good Norwegian dental care was.

I felt as though I'd had a workout; been put to the test and come through. Afterwards I went down to the bar and the barman shook my hand and said, 'You deserve a drink after that.'

'Thank you very much.'

He poured me a lager and said, 'That's £3.50.'

The Norwegians welcomed me at their table. They had been to Ireland and now they were touring Scotland. 'Are you from England?' one asked.

'Yes.'

Then she leant forward. 'Can I ask you something?'

'Sure.'

'It's a personal question.'

'OK.'

'Do the Scottish hate the English as much as they say?'

As I left, one of the smokers outside grabbed me. 'That was brilliant!'

'Thank you.' He was a bit drunk, but so what.

'I said brilliant.'

'Thank you.'

'You ... are the best ... kazoo player I've ever heard.'

I was ready for Edinburgh.

chapter twelve

the uke of edinburgh

The line goes: London is in England, Cardiff is in Wales and Edinburgh is in August. Arriving at Waverley Station at midnight this didn't seem like such a joke.

The sound of a calypso band drew me up through the narrow streets. I was led to an open-air bar, filled with yellow umbrellas and people drinking cool beer on a summer's night. It was like being back in Brighton but with better architecture.

Over-excited performers bumped into each other straight out of their shows. 'How was your first night?'

'Just fabulous. How was yours?'

'We aced them!'

Meanwhile post-show audiences, on their third drink, screamed at each other, 'You must see this show; the audience gets into bed; we had to literally get into bed. Literally. Like, a bed!'

All surfaces were plastered with posters advertising events for the coming month. Every spare floor space had been made available as a venue. 'Seriously, the play was upstairs in a clothing store!'

Some shows didn't even have a venue and took place walking around the city. For four weeks everything revolved around the festival and you really could be forgiven for thinking that come September the city was rolled up and put into storage.

It was notoriously difficult to find accommodation at festival-time, but I had a place to stay: my son was a student in Edinburgh. He was away, but this meant I had a nice big room overlooking the Meadows.

I had an urge to trash the place, use all the towels and leave them in a wet heap on the bedroom floor; then dirty every dish and not put one of them in the dishwasher. In the end I amused myself by wearing his clothes. His T-shirts fitted me now I'd lost so much weight. I was able to walk into town the following morning wearing a bright yellow shirt that said: *Round Britain Hitchhike 2009*.

Publicity is key in Edinburgh. You think the pavements are packed because of all the visitors, but it's because there are so many people handing out flyers. Walking up the Royal Mile is a show in itself as performers pitch their productions to you. Some address you from above on stilts, some sing their sales, others are dressed in suits and so polite. 'Maybe I could recommend a show for you this evening if you're looking for entertainment.' All of them are trying to do one thing – get you to take a flyer. I saw a Japanese woman politely taking one from all who offered. When she had so many she couldn't carry them, she just as politely dumped them in a skip.

It was the competition that was so overwhelming. Any performer needs an edge, but in Edinburgh your edge needed an edge. One comedian sang a song called 'I'm Glad John Lennon Died', which made people groan, but was, in fact, a very amusing grumble at the way your favourite rock stars, if they lived long enough, eventually made rubbish. More importantly it got him talked about.

Many performers were so keen to publicize themselves they did short day-time shows for free. At any time you could walk into one of the labyrinthine bars and find comedians queuing up to do a slot in a space no bigger than a sitting room. Even free shows were in competition with each other. Maybe the next step was to pay punters to come to see your act. Give the audience £2 each as they came in, concessions £2.50.

It was like a gold rush town. The sun came out and suddenly there was no sunscreen in the shops. There were queues at all the cash machines. The practice was for local people to rent out their homes for a huge amount and leave for the month as the city doubled in population. I saw a driver in a queue of traffic open her window and she called out to me for directions. 'Sorry, I'm a visitor,' I said. She drove slowly down the street, asking anyone she saw, and no one was able to help her. They all gave an out-of-town shrug.

I watched a woman with a staple gun attack a wooden hoarding with posters for her show, covering a sign that said: *stick no posters here*, and I really wondered if I had the balls for this place.

I couldn't begin to see how one man and his ukulele was ever going to get to play anywhere, less make an impact. I thought I might be able to busk, but that was heavily regulated, all sites designated, and apparently you needed a licence. Also, all the buskers in Edinburgh were brilliant. I came across one other ukulele player on the Royal Mile and not only could he play really well, he could also juggle with fire, ride a unicycle and do back flips.

A poetry open mic was advertised, and I went along in case they had room for a musical interlude. It was held in a tiny pub, long and thin. A sign on the door said, *Performance in progress, enter quietly.* I entered as quietly as I could, closed the door behind me and found myself standing next to the poet.

Having the stage right by the door seemed awkward, but poetry open mics are very different from their musical counterparts. They are a lot more serious; everyone listens very carefully. You wouldn't dare look at your phone. One woman read her poems in a manner that made them sound like instructions for assembling furniture from IKEA, which was actually very effective. Another woman read out a rambling story about going to the supermarket to do the weekly shopping. Its lack of structure became its structure. It was as if she was picking words out of a trolley at the checkout.

The woman sitting across from me said, 'Are you going to read something?'

'No.'

'Go on. Have a go.'

'I've nothing to read. I'm not a poet.'

'They don't get many men.'

What was she talking about? A man my age was getting up on the stage as she spoke. He announced he was going to read from his latest collection, and with his head at an angle like a puppy dog, he recited a series of paeons to man's search for love in later life, which seemed to me nothing more than an account of how he fancied younger women. All the other poets applauded, but surely they didn't like this stuff?

'What did you think of that?' I asked my neighbour.

'Poets are very supportive.'

The thing was, in a music open mic it was pretty easy to tell who was the next David Bowie and who wasn't. In the poetry equivalent no one had a clue.

Then I found a music open mic, in the Ale House on Clerk Street. I turned up early, assuming it would be buzzing, and it was certainly a packed house with a long list of players, but it was another of those irredeemably noisy bars where the performers were just an annoyance in the corner.

There was a good violinist, an interesting mandolin player, and a woman playing her flute with style. We were all playing our socks off to try to get some attention, but there was a first-day-back-at-school feel to the evening; the pub was full of people who had just arrived in town and had a year's worth of catching up to do. We were playing to their backs.

I did meet another ukulele player, though. Like me he'd just arrived. He was into reggae. 'Just hoping to play around a bit. You know. The ukulele is king in Edinburgh.'

He was right. Any performer was liable to produce a ukulele. Every comic would use one if he wanted a musical joke. It should have made me feel at home, but it did the opposite. I preferred it when I was the only ukulele player in town. Novelty appeal was what I depended on.

Because Edinburgh was such a free-for-all it was easy to get derailed. Were the couple having an argument in the café for real, or were they part of a play? Were the other people in the café the audience? Was I the audience? If so where could I buy a programme to see what I was watching?

I met a man from Blackburn and he said, 'I come from the North, but a Scottish comedian told me that up here I'm from the South. I hate coming from the South.'

To begin with I decided it was a bad idea to analyse anything too closely; best to take everything at face value. But then I went to see a play called *One Million Tiny Plays About Britain*, and that convinced me to do precisely the opposite.

The play comprised a series of vignettes, minute-long snatches of dialogue from a miscellany of lives: two workmen collecting litter in a park in Glasgow debating what constitutes treasure; a couple so desperate to get on the property ladder they consider putting in a lower offer on a house where there's been a murder; a man reading more into his leaving card than his female colleague intended. For two hours the audience eavesdropped on brief but intimate moments that told many random stories, but also one all-embracing one: everybody has a reason for being the way they are.

It was a simple but honest message, and one that immediately made me re-think my whole journey. I'd met so many people since Brighton. I had witnessed a million tiny plays myself: the Christians in Llandudno; the woman at the B&B in York with the dodgy toilet; the man in the library in Birkenhead who wanted to headbutt his computer. The people I had met had given my journey substance, but I had judged them entirely on the impact they had on me, not considering what might be driving their behaviour. Damn it! Now I would have to start all over again and treat people differently.

After the performance no one could say anything to me without me not-judging them. A car honked as I jumped a traffic light. I could have snarled back at the driver, instead I wondered what had put him in such a mood. Not just a dozy pedestrian. More likely a failing marriage, or being passed over for promotion, or the cosmetic surgery he was beginning to wish he'd never had?

But then, why was I being so non-judgemental? What was at the root of my change in behaviour? It wasn't just going to the play. That was merely the trigger ...

This is what happens to you if you overdose on the Fringe at Edinburgh. The surreal becomes real. A bald man in a collar and tie handed me a flyer for a show. There was something familiar about him. Oh yeah, he looked vaguely like John Malkovich. The flyer was for a show about Harold Pinter with Jude Law, directed by John Malkovich.

At that point I decided that, in such company, I was never going to make any impact on Edinburgh. And, of course, as soon as I said that the opposite was bound to happen.

THE UKE OF WALLINGTON

A little further down the street from John Malkovich, I was handed another flyer. This one was for a show called *Tricity Vogue's Ukulele Cabaret*.

It took place that evening at the Three Sisters. It was free and promised the chance to see the 'brightest stars strut their stuff'. I didn't know what to expect, but I took my uke along just in case.

Tricity Vogue had made a name for herself on the Fringe scene as a champion of the ukulele, and she brought her cabaret to Edinburgh each festival. She was an unusual woman, and not just because she had named herself after a 1960s electric oven. She wore an evening dress, a feather fascinator, high heels and long black gloves. Oh, and let's not forget the ukulele wired to her head. Quite how it was secured up there wasn't clear, but she sashayed onto the stage looking like she'd stepped straight out of a cartoon.

The Three Sisters was a large bar. There were probably a hundred people in, all up for a good time on this first weekend of the festival. They weren't hard to win over and were keen to volunteer when Tricity asked for judges – because the show was a competition. The prize was the title 'The Uke of Edinburgh'.

A number of performers from other shows in the festival had been invited to play, most of them comedians who used a ukulele in their act. The idea was that they played a couple of tunes and were awarded points by the panel of audience judges. At the end of the show the highest score became the U of E.

But that wasn't the only reward. The real prize of the night for the lucky winner was an invitation to play the ukulele on Tricity Vogue's head.

What chemical she had been taking when she came up with this format is anyone's guess, but hey, this was the Edinburgh Fringe and there were far stranger shows than this, probably on the same street. The audience were game anyway. Tricity played a song to get them going and then invited the first performer on stage.

He was good. He was funny. He wore a funny hat and a bright shirt. He was very hairy as well, but in a good way. He may not have been aware of it, but as he was playing you kept thinking: that guy is hirsute, give him a round of applause.

The panel weren't so easily impressed. Out of 10, he got a few sevens, a five, a couple of fours. They weren't giving it away.

Next up was a duo whose show was based around vegetable gardening. They played songs about slugs and about fooling around in the greenhouse with Alan Titchmarsh. They went down well, and got mostly sevens and eights.

Next came a woman who sang a song that was graphic in its description of oral sex. The audience was appalled. Not by the subject matter, but by the fact that she was playing a six-string ukulele, which is really just a small guitar. She was funny, but her lack of respect for the instrument brought her marks down.

I had kept my ukulele concealed in a bag, unsure at the start of what I might be letting myself in for. But, having seen a few acts, I got it into my head that I could do just as well. Sensible voice said: don't be so stupid, keep it in the bag. Senseless voice said: you've come a long way, get it out and ask to play.

I actually decided to toss for it. I took out a coin and said, heads you ask, tails you don't. It came up tails, but then I went ahead and asked anyway.

I wondered if Tricity would, as politely as possible, call security. Couldn't I see this was a professionally run show and didn't depend on wannabe players like me?

But she didn't say that. She said, 'Sure, you're on next.'

I didn't have time to feel nervous. Before I knew it, I was up on the stage under very bright lights. The bar and audience suddenly seemed more the size of Wembley Arena. Something was keeping me standing upright, but I wasn't sure what.

I told them the truth. For the first time I told an audience I was on an open-mic tour. I had come up from Brighton and I was heading to Cape Wrath, and I wanted to play in a show at the Edinburgh Festival just to say I'd done it. 'So here goes. Chuck Berry song.'

I can't remember much. Just that I got a bit carried away at one point and strummed the ukulele like Pete Townshend. When the kazoo solo came I recalled what the drunk man in Stirling had said ('You're the best kazoo player I've ever ever heard') and as I was playing I thought: if only Miles Davis's parents had bought him a kazoo instead of a trumpet, well, who knows.

I finished the song. The place erupted. I was about to get down when I heard someone shout. 'More!' I peered into the lights, trying to make sure it wasn't a member of my family.

'More!' someone else shouted.

This was it. At last, a genuine encore. 'You ain't nothin' but a hound dog,' I sang and everyone joined in.

My soul wasn't quite bare up there that night, but I'd say it was topless at least. And the audience responded. I looked up and saw some people holding their phones. They couldn't all be checking emails. Some of them were taking pictures.

Afterwards I held my ukulele aloft like Paganini held his violin, and I bathed in the applause. There was a tear in my eye and a thump in my chest, and when Tricity asked the audience for votes, I knew how Bucks Fizz felt at *Eurovision*.

I needn't have worried. All the judges gave me 10 except for one misery who only gave me a nine. At first, I thought I was getting the sympathy vote, but then I decided no, it was the empathy vote. I won because they thought: if he can do that, then so can I. I was the people's champ, and at that moment, all those times in my life when music had failed me – like when I choked on my plectrum and had to be slapped on the back by the bass player – they dissolved into insignificance. This was what all my musical endeavour had been building up to. I was the Uke of Edinburgh and all the pain had been worth it.

Now came the real prize. The chance to play the ukulele on Tricity's head. It was all a bit clumsy to be honest, a fumbling. I bent down then she bent down in front of me, then I confessed I was left-handed and couldn't play it unless she turned round. In the end I tried to put my arms around her head without touching her. I fingered the fretboard, strummed a chord and experienced a strange thrill that I don't really want to experience again. Finally, all the performers were asked on stage and we played a song together, which reminded me of *Sunday Night at the London Palladium* except we weren't going round and round.

Afterwards, I was given a Uke of Edinburgh badge, and Tricity said, 'So where else are you playing?'

'Nowhere.'

As I spoke, one of the other performers asked me to come and play at a lunchtime show he was hosting the following day. 'Family show. You'll go down a treat.'

'You're going to have a great festival,' said Tricity.

I should have left Edinburgh that night, gone back to the flat, packed my bag and taken a night bus north with the knowledge that, had I wanted to, I could have had a great festival – Tricity Vogue had said so herself.

But I'd been seduced. The Edinburgh Festival's easy, I said to myself as I strode home, U of E badge proudly displayed on my chest. What was all the fuss about? And I started thinking about getting an act together and coming back the following year with a one-man show of my own and standing on the Royal Mile handing out leaflets.

It was a delusion that lasted until the following lunchtime, when I kept my date and turned up to play the family show. There were six performers and an audience of four: a family with two young kids. My experience over the summer had shown me that having more people on stage than in the audience, while not a good thing, isn't necessarily the death of a show. But then halfway through my set the family got up and left. 'Sorry,' said the dad. 'We've got tickets for *Sheep Ahoy!*'

You couldn't blame them. *Sheep Ahoy!* sounded like fun. 'Can't understand it,' said Chris who had invited me. 'We had at least 15 in yesterday.'

I didn't let it get me down. I had had my night of triumph. Edinburgh had been a defining moment. From now on, if I had another one of my panics, when the whole idea of this trip seemed ridiculous, when I put my hands to my head and said, 'What do you think you're doing?' I had only to look at my badge for an answer: the Uke of Edinburgh.

chapter thirteen

ullapool unplugged

'He's going very fast,' said the passenger next to me on the bus to Aberdeen.

He was quite right. The driver had his foot on the floor, and was bombing up a dual carriageway in the fast lane. I hadn't noticed; I was used to Formula One bus drivers. I thought: this is nothing, you should catch the 68 out of Winchester.

'There's a severe weather warning as well,' said my neighbour.

The rain had started the day before and hadn't stopped. Now it was lashing down as the driver overtook a truck.

The truth was, I was happy to be speeding north. With Edinburgh behind me, the Highlands were on the map now, and they covered a vast space. This was the last leg of the journey, but also the wildest and most remote. The towns were sparse, the roads long, and Cape Wrath looked many miles away.

'There's a tree come down in Lanarkshire,' my neighbour added and folded his newspaper. 'A motorist taken to hospital.'

It was a grey Sunday and I was approaching another grey city, Aberdeen, which, in fact, takes pride on how grey it looks. It has labelled itself the Granite City and on a day like this I was probably seeing it at its greyest. I should have considered myself lucky.

I expected it to be closed and quiet, but the main street was busy and all the shops open. A newsagents had a sign stuck in the window written in felt-tip: *Bargain Umbrellas £5. Multi colours.*

There was a large police presence for the Aberdeen–Celtic match that had kicked off earlier. 'What was the score?' I asked a man in a green-hooped jersey standing outside a pub. 'One nil to Celtic,' he bawled. He was in heaven. He had a pint in one hand, a cigarette in the other and behind him in the bar a live Irish band celebrating his team's win.

I planned to play in a local pub myself that night and, as usual, I had a couple of hours to kill. When the rain stopped I walked down to the seafront where there was a good sandy beach and the usual amusements, the sort of arcades that look so gloomy the minute the sun goes in.

More in keeping with the steely day were the big vessels, ferry-size monsters that were sailing out of the docks to sea. 'Oil rig supply boats,' said a man sitting by the harbour in an overcoat.

Aberdeen was the shore base of the British oil industry and for years had been known as a boomtown, but now the rigs were being decommissioned. 'Costs as much to pull them down as it did to build them.'

The city still made its living out of oil, but was trying to prepare for an oil-less future. 'There's no fishing industry,' said my friend. As he spoke, a fishing boat chugged past, but it looked like a toy compared to the supply boats.

There was once a tourist industry, but by the look of it that too had run dry. I said, 'It's a bit grey for a tourist town.'

'It's no grey. It's silver. Aberdeen is the Silver City with Golden Sands.'

The rain started again. The North Sea had never looked grimmer. It was mid-August and if I'd come here for a beach holiday with my family, I would have abandoned them and joined the Celtic fan in the pub.

I found a place to stay in a granite terrace on the edge of town. This stone didn't seem to weather at all, and so all the houses in Aberdeen looked as though they'd been built a few years ago instead of a hundred. 'Are you in oil?' said the B&B owner.

'No. Just passing through.'

'Most people who stay here are in the oil.' She stopped a young man on the stairs as he was walking out. 'This chap works in the oil. Don't you?'

He spoke with a Scandinavian accent. He said his job was to do with valves and seals. He explained it very slowly and at great length, and the landlady and I listened and nodded, and then when he'd left neither of us could think of any intelligent comment to make. 'He's Norwegian,' she said.

When people weren't dealing with the oil in Aberdeen they were dealing with Donald Trump. He was building a golf course further up the coast, having made world news with his plan to bulldoze the coastal habitat, and his battle with a local old-timer who wouldn't sell his land, no matter how much money was offered.

It was all good copy and now Trump was back in the news because he was objecting to a proposed wind farm out at sea. Presumably, he didn't want his hotel guests to have to look out on anything so unsightly, although personally I'd have been grateful for anything that could break up the view of the North Sea. One man said to me, 'If there was a wind farm, it would have to be maintained. Aberdeen would become a wind farm boomtown then.'

That sounded a little optimistic. But the search for the next generation of jobs was a real one and I suspected that most people wanted Trump's hotel and golf course development to go ahead because it would offer local employment. But they weren't going to give him the pleasure of knowing that.

The open mic for the evening was in a pub called the Globe. There were a number of post-football match drinkers at the bar and a grumpy host running the show who didn't looked thrilled when I asked if I could play. I wanted to say, 'Do you know who I am? I am the Uke of Edinburgh.'

A man with a red balloon of a face opened the proceedings and played some good blues with a voice as solid as the local stone. The audience wanted more, but he wanted more to drink and there was only ever going to one winner in that battle.

The host stepped in and played as if he was under contractual obligation; and then a local girl followed him playing some of her own songs. The highlight of the evening, though, was a middle-aged man named Alan, who took the stage with a bright red Fender guitar and gave us a Shadows recital.

He played all the hits – 'Wonderful Land', 'Apache', 'Walk, Don't Run' – and although he didn't do the funny Shadows walk, he stood there in his shirtsleeves and glasses and it didn't matter what anyone thought, he was Hank Marvin.

He stood out because he was having such a good time, and also because he was sober. When it was my turn to play, a man rolled over to me, shouting, 'I'm Davie Davidson the vocalist, pleased to meet you,' and then he tripped over a cable and fell against the amps.

He wanted to play next, but he needed to borrow a guitar and the host refused to lend him his. 'I never lend my guitar to someone who's had too much to drink,' he said, which ruled out most of the Globe.

I went and spoke to Alan. Open mics were made for people like him. For 15 minutes every Sunday night he got to step up on stage and become his hero. He'd been playing since he was 10 years old, he said, 'ever since I heard "Apache"'. His Fender was a genuine model, 'Fiesta Red', and his amp was a Vox AC30. 'Just like Hank used to use.'

He regularly went to Shadows conventions. 'I've got a job looking at computers all day,' he said, as if that explained everything. I suggested he should recruit a drummer and bass player, become a Shadows tribute band. Sometimes he did just that, he said, but 'they want singers, the pubs do.'

As he spoke, the 'vocalist' Davie Davidson, having managed to borrow a guitar from somewhere, was on stage bumping into things trying to sing a Neil Young song. It was all a bit sad. Edinburgh seemed an age ago, and I felt the urge to get to Cape Wrath where the audience at the Smoo Cave Hotel would be discerning and appreciative and where there was probably a welcome banner up already.

The severe weather warning was still in place the following day. The rain ran down the granite and the wind attacked TV aerials. In a bin I saw one of the bargain umbrellas, its veins bent and broken, not up to the job.

I had phoned the Smoo Cave Hotel to let them know where I was, and ask the best way of getting there. The manager said there was one bus a day from Ullapool.

'What time do you want me there?' I asked.

'Whenever.'

'Maybe start about 8.30?'

'Fine.'

'Play for about 30, 45 minutes.'

'Fine.'

'You could tell the local paper if you want.'

'Tell them what?'

'You can bill me as the Uke of Edinburgh.'

'The what?'

'Nothing.'

Ullapool was a good distance away, but I worked out I could get there by public transport in a day. The route was via Inverness and that was a four-hour bus journey itself, so I decided to treat myself to a train. It was double the price but half the time.

The train ended up taking four-and-a-half hours. A few miles west from Aberdeen the line was flooded and we were transferred onto buses. But the roads were flooded as well. The route through to Elgin where we could reconnect with a train was one big traffic jam.

The passengers were all very stoical. Somebody at the back started to sing in Gaelic. One man called out crossword clues. The woman behind me spoke on the phone. 'I'm on a bus now. I was on the train, but now I'm on a bus. Be back on the train in a bit.'

It was the little girl across the aisle I was most concerned about. 'Are you all right?' her mother kept asking her. She nodded, but she looked green. 'You don't feel sick?' said her mother.

I thought: stop putting ideas in her head.

'Cos you look like you're going to be sick. See if I've got a bag.'

She hunted round in her luggage for a sick bag but couldn't find one. I wondered if I had anything to offer. The only container I could think of was the sun hat I had bought in the charity shop in Shropshire. I'd had it for 500 miles, but would happily have sacrificed it if it meant avoiding a stream of vomit running down the aisle.

We got to Elgin and waited there another hour. Another mother and child were having a difficult time. The little boy was so bored he was trying to chew his foot. He slid down his seat to the floor. 'Jack, come here!' said his mother, but he was past hearing her. She didn't know what to do with him. She had a baby to look after as well. She looked at me and tried to smile, but I could see desperation.

The boy lay on the floor by my bag. He saw the mitten on top of my ukulele.

'What's that?'

'Have a guess.'

He looked at me suspiciously. 'What is it?'

'See if you can guess.'

He looked at his mother. 'Have a guess,' she said.

'Don't know.'

'All right you can touch it, gently.'

He poked the ukulele. 'It's a shoe.'

'No. Try again.'

'It's a shoe.'

'It's not a shoe.'

By this time other passengers were taking an interest. Just what did I have in my bag under the mitten?

'Take it off,' said the little boy.

So I took the mitten off and showed him the top of the ukulele.

'Now do you know what it is?'

He shook his head. I took the whole ukulele out and put it round his neck. He sat down next to me and I told him to strum the strings while I played the chords.

'When's your birthday?'

He looked at his mum. 'November,' she said.

'This is for November.'

And we played 'Happy Birthday'. His mum joined in. 'Happy Birthday, dear Jack, Happy Birthday to you!'

The passengers applauded. Jack beamed. A little girl further down the row said, 'It's my birthday in April.'

The train arrived and we crawled into Inverness. There, in a café, I heard the radio weather forecast. It said it was raining. It was as though the forecaster had just looked out of the window. But he didn't stop there. It was going to rain for three more days, he said, and be cold, and windy. I shivered in my seat. Getting to the end of this journey didn't sound like it was going to be fun.

There were only four people on the bus from Inverness. We quickly entered wild country. Foaming waterfalls tumbled down mountainsides. What few trees there were all leant one way, clinging on. Even the sheep looked as though they could use a break.

Donald McDonald remembered the Klondike period in Ullapool with a shake of the head. 'Everyone made money. Some made lots of money.'

It was in the late seventies. From August to March every year factory ships from the Eastern Bloc would anchor in Loch Broom. They came for the mackerel, and the local fishermen worked all hours to supply them. Donald was an agent for a number of local boats. 'They made more money than they'd ever see again.' But the work took its toll. 'Lots of money, but lots of stress. Many of them died early.'

He was retired now and he helped his wife run the B&B. 'Look at me, a tough fisherman, laying the breakfast table.'

His sons had carried on where he left off. 'They're well educated – qualified to do all sorts. But you can't stop them going to sea. It's in the blood.'

He spoke as if he thought he'd had too much luck. He'd survived a life sailing up and down the Minch; he had a nice house and a nice car. But he was vulnerable again now his sons were out there. 'They're cocky. Like I was. You think you know the sea, but you'll never know it as well as the ocean.'

There was good food in Ullapool, good fish and chips, and, in one restaurant, scallops and black pudding on the menu, which looked like a dare. 'Stornoway black pudding,' said the waitress. 'It's the finest.'

I didn't think there could be such a thing as fine black pudding, but I tried it and she was right. It was the best food I'd had on the whole trip. 'Fantastic,' I said to her. 'Where's the chef from?'

'I don't know. I'll go and ask.'

Before I could explain it was just a line, she'd gone back into the kitchen. 'Where's Derek from?' I heard her shout.

She came back out. 'He's from Carlisle.'

'Carlisle. Good. Thanks.'

I wandered round the village at twilight and watched the low cloud try to clear the hills on the other side of the loch. The midges were out. A family on holiday lined up and dad sprayed them one by one.

The main street in Ullapool was the harbour front and everything leant towards the port. There was still a small fishing fleet, but now the village was better known as a ferry terminal with its link to Lewis in the Outer Hebrides. There were travellers from all over Europe here – Spanish, Dutch, Italian, French – all waiting for a boat. It was like a transit lounge. I went to the Argyll Hotel later where I'd been told there was an open mic and it was as polyglot as a bar in a border town.

The music was already under way when I got there, but this was nothing like the entertainment I'd been used to. All the performers sat at a table in the middle of the bar, and took it in turns. If you wanted to join in, you did. There was no sound equipment.

The audience was encouraged to contribute songs as well, and that made it a more inclusive event than any of the open mics I'd played at all the way up England. I'd been told that once I got into the Highlands this sort of thing might happen, and that they might frown on anything that wasn't traditional Scottish music. But the audience in the Argyll was so international that the music followed suit. An American played bluegrass. A Scotsman sang unaccompanied in Gaelic. Another local sang a self-penned ode to his dog who was sitting on the seat next to him. A German in the audience announced, 'I know one song in English: "Soldier, soldier, will you marry me with your musket, fife and drum?".' When I chipped in with a Nick Lowe song, I felt as foreign as anyone else.

A Spanish woman said to me, 'That song you played.'

'Nick Lowe. "Half A Man".'

'What are the words?'

'"You'd better run, you'd better hide. You'd better lock your house and keep the kids inside."'

'Yes?'

'"Here comes the 20th-century's latest scam. He's half a boy and half a man."'

'Yes?'

'Yes.'

'What does it mean?'

'It's a song ... about ... I haven't got a clue what it means.'

The evening was wrapped up with a rendition of 'Scotland The Brave', which the whole pub sang even though only the bar staff knew the words. My Spanish friend said to me, 'The Scottish enjoy themselves very much.'

'Aye,' I said.

'Are you Scottish?'

'No.'

'English?'

'Yes.'

She looked disapproving. She just said, 'The riots.'

Donald McDonald said the same thing the following morning as he fussed over breakfast, 'There's been more riots; you'll want the television on?'

He rummaged around for the TV remote, then when he found it he couldn't find the right button. 'I can do 30 words a minute Morse code, but I can't work out how to switch on the blasted TV.'

The news was appalling. London was ablaze, so were Bristol, Liverpool and Manchester, all places I had passed through in the last few weeks. In Liverpool I had seen what seemed like half the city gather with pride to celebrate the opening of its new museum and now they were looting the place. The Scottish media was keen to distance itself. This was an English problem. It wasn't happening in Glasgow.

Donald was even more detached. 'Oh well,' he said. 'Let's see what the weather's like.'

His reaction was understandable. Being up here in this beautiful, isolated place, such bad behaviour must have seemed alien, as if it was all happening on the other side of the world. The weather in the Minch was more important.

'Where are you heading?'

'Cape Wrath.'

'Now there's a place they named well.'

The familiar red, white and black CalMac ferry steamed in down the loch, and Ullapool shifted into gear. The quayside came to life: the gulls grew excited; the dock workers pulled their gloves on; the travellers gathered up their baggage. Hi-viz jackets appeared everywhere.

It went like clockwork. The boat docked and quickly decanted the town's new set of visitors. The exiting ones walked up the gangplank. Cars drove into the belly. Stores were taken on. Ropes were cast off and then she backed out like a bus and headed off down the loch again, looking stately and dependable as she disappeared round the headland.

Peace returned, the gulls quietened down. The new visitors checked into the camp site. The only things moving were the clouds as they swirled around the distant peaks. This was a routine that never changed. No one wanted it to. It was a daily ritual and it gave the village its purpose.

The bus to Durness – the nearest village to Cape Wrath – met the boat, and it quickly filled with Europeans. 'The exchange rate is very good,' a Dutch woman explained to me.

'Have you been to England as well?' I asked.

'England has got riots,' she said. 'You are English?'

I wanted them to think I was Scottish, but they could always tell. In fact there were no Scottish people on the bus. Only the driver.

It was five hours to Durness. The weather got worse as we drove up the coast, windy with squalls of rain. I noted that everyone else was dressed for the Arctic.

The driver wanted to be our guide. 'Anything you want to know about the area, just ask.' No one had any questions, so he asked them himself, then gave the answers. 'People often enquire about the Geopark and the Moine Thrust Belt,' he said. Most on the bus were keen to get some sleep, having been up on the boat all night. Instead they were treated to a lecture on tectonic plate theory. 'The oldest rocks in Europe!' He looked appalled we weren't more excited.

It was certainly hard and barren country we were passing through, moorland with craggy hills in the distance. There were no trees at all, or habitation. It was as if humans couldn't survive out there and we were only breathing because we were in the bubble of the bus. When we finally reached Lochinver, it felt like a stage coach station.

'Statutory break. Forty-five minutes,' said the driver. 'There's a café, and a visitor centre opened in 1995 by Magnus Magnusson.'

There were banners in Lochinver advertising the annual Highland Games. 'Village is full to the brim,' said the woman in her garden, proudly hanging a *No Vacancies* sign beneath her B&B notice. 'Everyone comes home for the games.'

The only place that was empty was the café. 'What games?' said the woman making tea.

'The Highland Games,' I said. 'Everyone's very excited, apparently.'

'They haven't lived up here long enough,' she grumbled. 'It's all the new people. All the English. They like to see Tossing the Caber and all that stuff.'

A Scotsman flagged down the bus not far from Lochinver. He looked as though he'd been living wild for weeks. He was covered in bites and smelt of someone who has been wet for too long. In fact he'd only been out two nights.

'I camped in a bad place,' he said to me. 'My tent's not very good. I borrowed it from a friend at work.'

He was a kitchen porter from Inverness; once a year he came out on a camping and hiking trip to the Highlands. 'Puts me back in touch. Lets me have a think.' His marriage had failed but he lived near his daughter and we swapped stories of raising teenagers. She was going to university and that made him very proud. He wanted her to come with him on one of his camping trips some time; he wanted to show her the real Scotland.

'She likes hiking?' I asked.

'She prefers the craft shops.'

He'd been to Sandwood Bay, the legendary Sutherland beach known as the 'most beautiful in Britain', accessible only after a four-mile hike over the moors.

'I've never been,' I said.

'I wouldn't bother. It was packed. Groups of them hiking in. Butlins.'

His idea of 'packed' was probably different from mine, although I had heard stories like this about Sandwood Bay, as if the minute somewhere gets labelled the 'most beautiful' it's destined to lose what made it the most beautiful in the first place.

I thought he was through with his trip, that the weather had beaten him, but an hour down the road he called out to the driver to stop, and he got out in an utterly desolate spot, surrounded by mountains and moorland with no sign of shelter anywhere, and the clouds thrashing about over his head.

He waved, then swung his rucksack on his back and walked off. He gave the impression he came here to find himself, but he'd be lucky to find anything out there.

The bus pressed on along the single-track road, everyone quiet as the mountains closed in. The driver had tried to impress us with facts, but there was no need. The landscape itself had left us speechless.

This was like nothing I'd seen in Britain before. If these were the oldest rocks in Europe, they looked like it. It was as though we were travelling through a prehistoric land, somewhere mythical. There was a definite sense we were heading towards the end of something. But not just Britain. This little bus was driving us along the road to the end of the world.

cape wrath – one night only

There was an outboard ferry across the Kyle of Durness to the Cape Wrath Peninsula. I knew the ferryman was called John because Donald McDonald had told me to say hello. 'He's called Dark John,' Donald had said. 'Left over from the Armada.'

That was an old story – everyone on the Scottish (or Irish) coast with a dark complexion was a lander from the Armada.

I told the ferryman Donald sent his best wishes. He said, 'Oh yes, I know Duncan.'

'Donald.'

'Donald. Fine young man.'

'He's late seventies.'

'I haven't seen him for a while.'

John took me and a boat full of Italians and French across the inlet. A minibus was waiting on the other side. 'It's 12 miles to the lighthouse,' said the driver. 'You can walk it if you want. But remember it's 12 back.'

We all clambered onto the bus and set off along the rough track. I sat next to a French lady. 'You are English?' she said.

How could everyone tell I was English so easily? Was it really that obvious?

She had been travelling round Scotland for two months. 'The Highlanders say they don't like the Lowlanders much. But you know who they really don't like?'

'Don't tell me. The English?'

'The English,' and she giggled.

I assured her it was just traditional for the Scottish to hate the English. It wasn't actually true. I asked her where else she'd been. 'Ireland,' she said. 'They really *do* hate the English.'

The bus driver had written a book about the Cape. 'Everything you need to know and more besides!' he announced, and waved a copy at us. He had a military manner. If he wanted our attention, to tell us interesting anecdotes with amusing endings, he just stopped the bus and waited until we were listening. In the middle of the moor he pointed to a wreck of an army tank painted pink, and explained how the Cape was a Ministry of Defence firing range and the wrecked pink tank was for target practice. 'Don't know why it's painted pink. Probably belonged to the Queen's Regiment.'

There was a whooshing noise as the quip went straight over the heads of the various nationalities on board. 'Don't think they got that one,' he said to me.

It wasn't that long ago there was a community out on the Cape. There were lighthouse personnel, and shepherds and their families. As recently as the 1930s there was a school with 10 children. But over the years they drifted away to less isolated places, and now the landscape was so empty that any feature, like a derelict cottage, took on significance.

We bumped along across the moor in silence. There were golden eagles and red deer, the highest cliffs on mainland Britain and giant rock stacks offshore. The weather was blown in ceaselessly from the sea and dumped as if a delivery was being made, to be dispersed from here to all corners of the nation. Here's your weather for the week. Pass it round.

The level of suspense was rising. We knew what we were going to see – we had all looked at the pictures – but we also knew that we were coming to the end of the road. And there was a thrill in that.

Then we came over a rise and there it was: the lighthouse and the real-life 90-degree turn of the coastline; the huge cliffs and beyond, the icy, writhing sea. I tried to put myself in a suitable frame of mind. This was the end of my journey. My goal. I wanted to feel emotional. 'I've come all the way from Brighton,' I announced to my French friend.

She looked at me oddly. 'I've come from Paris.'

Well, of course she had.

The clouds cleared and there were views all down the coast. The cliffs were sheer and brutal. Below them the two seas came crashing together like heavyweight boxers, spray flying, violent and relentless. Just offshore wild islands of rock were pounded tirelessly by the waves. Two hundred years ago, three ships were wrecked in one night out there. After that it was decided a lighthouse should be built.

The light is computerized now, of course, and there's even a café for visitors in the outbuildings. But this is still a very wild spot. Like everyone else – including Donald McDonald – I had thought it was named for the angry seas below, but Wrath, in this case, comes from the Viking word *hvarf*, which means 'turning point'. It was where the Viking boats turned east to head for home.

I stood as near to the cliff edge as I dared. (When pressed, the minibus driver had told me that on two occasions he had taken one less passenger back than he had brought out.) I said to my French friend, 'Why have you come all the way to Cape Wrath?'

She shrugged. 'It's so far away.'

A little sailing boat rode the swell below. I took my second photograph of the whole trip. The sky was completely clear now. The weather had gone south. I peered out to the horizon. There was nothing left. This was the point where everyone turned.

I found a place to stay in a windswept bungalow on the edge of Durness. There was a wood fire in the living room and the kids were curled up on the couch watching TV.

'When do you go back to school?'

'Tuesday,' they chorused.

Outside, the wind blew a yellow plastic bag across the treeless farm. There was nothing in between the loch and the mountains beyond. Kids made their own entertainment in the summer holidays here. They did have just about the finest beach I'd ever seen in Britain right outside the back door, but that could get boring if you grew up with it.

'Not much to do round here for kids, is there?' I said to their mother.

'No. We had 26 pilot whales beach in the loch couple of months ago. But they all died.'

I went for a walk along the sands. I needed to plan my concert. Six weeks on the road, but I was feeling more nervous about the Smoo Cave gig than any of the others. I was on my own tonight.

My plan was to blend songs with hilarious but insightful stories from my journey. Chuck Berry and the thrill of evensong in Salisbury Cathedral. Buddy Holly and what it feels like to be the only tourist in Birkenhead. It was the last night of my tour. I wanted it to be one to remember.

I followed the curve of the magnificent Balnakeil Bay, acres of brilliant white sand with a carpet of marram grass rolling over the dunes. Any habitation here looked impossibly exposed, and yet there was a thriving craft community set back from the beach, housed in a series of Nissen huts from the days when there was an early-warning station on the headland. There was a potter, a wood turner, a chocolate factory and a variety of artists.

I came across a man who repaired musical instruments. He was Belgian and told me his name was Ludo, 'as in snakes and ladders'. He offered me a herb tea. 'Mint okay?' And he picked a mint leaf from the garden and poured some hot water on it.

We sat in the sun lounge with passion fruit growing all around us. 'We have so much daylight in the summer, you can grow anything.'

I couldn't understand how he could make a living repairing instruments up here, but he had the Highland schools contract. 'I drive to Inverness, fill the car with instruments and bring them back.' In his workshop a trombone lay on the table.

The question was, of course, how somebody ended up here in the first place, but his story was probably not unusual for Cape Wrath. Like everyone else, he had found himself at the end of the road, and instead of turning round, he stopped. He left once but came back and before he knew it, he'd been living here 30 years.

This was an outpost, but it wasn't hard to see the attraction. Ludo's partner was an artist and I bought one of her paper collages as a present for my wife. It depicted one tiny, isolated crofter's cottage on the shores of the loch with huge mountains and heavy weather behind. In a landscape like this you're constantly reminded of the immense power of the natural world. When you wake up every morning it doesn't matter which window you look out of, you can't help but feel you're a very small part of a much bigger picture.

Durness had been settled by people who had just turned up and stayed. They learnt how to live up here, which meant multi-tasking. I met a bus driver, but he didn't just drive the bus. He made jewellery; he was a mechanic; he was a tourist guide. 'John Lennon used to come on holiday here, you know.'

So even Cape Wrath had a Beatles link. What was that John Lennon said about being bigger than Jesus?

'He used to stay with his Aunt Elizabeth. She's buried

in the churchyard. It's all on the tour of Durness.'

The tour of Durness didn't take long. The highlight was the Smoo Cave, which was spectacular, a gaping hole in the limestone cliff where salt water met fresh in a furious subterranean waterfall. It was like peering at nature's dentistry with cavities everywhere, an open mouth to walk into.

But after that the only excitement was the threat of being run over by the boy racer with the bright orange Escort who drove up and down the single-track road, revving his engine and lunging at tourists. I leapt onto the verge as he passed me one way, then leapt again as he went for the kill on the way back. I'd come all the way from East Sussex; I didn't want to be run down in Durness.

I had a shower, put on the clean shirt I'd been saving, and headed off for the Smoo Cave Hotel. I hadn't seen it on my earlier ramblings so I asked directions. 'That way,' said an Italian family. 'Easy. You don't miss it.'

Somehow I missed it. I walked a mile out of town before I decided this wasn't right. How could you miss somewhere in Durness? It wasn't possible. I hurried back. I was going to be late now. The crowd would be growing restless, stamping its feet, slow hand clapping. 'Where is he? We've travelled miles for this.'

Somehow I'd walked past the signpost, *Smoo Cave Hotel This Way*. It pointed along a road towards the cliff. By the time I got there, I was sweating as well as nervous. I gathered myself outside, checked my fly, flattened my hair. I looked in the windows – no poster. So what? Word of mouth was what worked in places like this.

The first thing I noticed was a big TV in the lobby area with a football match on. Scotland were playing Denmark. The score was one all. The second thing I noticed was a big pool table in the middle of the bar with a group of local lads round it. They were loud and rowdy and probably having as much fun as it's possible to have with a game of pool.

The third thing I noticed was the audience, which consisted of John the ferryman and a couple of people eating dinner.

John shook my hand and then saw my ukulele. 'Oh. It's you is it?'

'It's me.'

'I didn't know it was you.'

'It's me all right.'

'I brought my box.'

He opened a big black case by his side and pulled out an accordion. Why had he bought that?

'She told us you were coming. Here's Ludo.'

Ludo the instrument repair man came in with a saxophone. Then a lad arrived with a box of harmonicas. I wasn't quite sure what was happening.

'Off you go then,' said John.

'What?'

'Do your ukulele.'

Not only was there no audience, there was nowhere to play. Every open mic I'd been to had a designated corner of the bar and a space cleared, but not here.

'Where shall I play?'

'Anywhere you like.'

I tried to position myself, but everywhere I stood the pool table was in between me and everyone else. 'Maybe we could move the pool table.'

'Ooh, the boys wouldn't like that.'

'I'll wait until they stop.'

'They'll be playing all night.'

He was right. There was a stack of 50p pieces on the table.

This wasn't going to plan. It wasn't supposed to be like this. I was supposed to be the centre of attention and have my audience enthralled.

There was nothing else I could do. I stood against the wall and started to play, dodging the pool cues as they shot back. There was no sound system and the pool players easily shouted me out every time one of them potted a ball. I just played on, feeling I was getting smaller with each song.

'That's very nice,' said John. 'Let us know when you want some help.'

He ordered another Guinness. I played another song. A roar from the other bar told us that Scotland had scored. A roar from the pool table told me that this wasn't going to work. I said to John, 'Maybe you'd like to join in now.'

And that was all it took.

Two hours later, we were still playing. By that time there were so many of us we'd overwhelmed the pool players.

John the ferryman pitched to and fro with his accordion like a sailor on deck. Ludo could improvise around anything on his sax. A guitarist who knew all the songs led the way. A pool player swapped his cue for a harmonica and joined in.

The pub had filled up nicely. A man tugged my arm and said, 'Would you mind if I played my melodeon?' He was an English visitor, a soulmate with zips in his trouser knees. 'I was told you were coming,' he said. 'I was told to come and play.'

The truth was the evening had been planned, just not in the way I'd expected. When the locals heard a ukulele player was coming, they weren't bothered how far he'd come, and the last thing on their minds was to sit politely and listen to his stories. They saw me simply as an excuse to have a good session.

A Czech barmaid joined in on guitar and vocals. She threw her head back and let go. The saxophone played a cool vibrato. John put down his accordion and picked up a Guinness. The melodeon player took over from him and stamped his feet. The harmonica player was the Howlin' Wolf of Cape Wrath. I strummed along on my ukulele, although I knew that no one could hear it above the din.

But that was okay. By then I'd realized that the evening wasn't about me. It was about them, and, if I stood back a bit, I could see that this had been the case for the whole of the trip.

I'd wanted this to be the rock 'n' roll tour I'd never had, and it had been that, but it had also been a tour of other people's music: the left-over hippy on the Isle of Wight, the chaoscillator player in Manchester, the woman singing 'Danny Boy' in Newcastle. From Brighton to Cape Wrath all sorts of people were making music, and I would remember their performances long after I'd forgotten my own.

The pub was never going to shut as long as there were people in it, and the people were never going to leave as long as the pub was open. Eventually Ludo gave me a lift back. He said, 'Shame you're not staying longer.' It was a shame. This was a unique place. I imagined myself staying two or three nights, getting a job in a bar, eventually opening the beach-combers museum I had always wanted to, and never leaving.

'We could play more music,' said Ludo, and he smiled. 'I like to play with the ukulele.' He was very kind. But people had been kind all along. The ukulele really did make them smile.

I got into bed and set my alarm. I needed to get up early to catch the bus to Lairg where I could pick up a southbound train.

A dog barked outside. A child coughed upstairs. I lay there a minute, wondering if I could hear the sea.

This wasn't really the end of the road. The Faroe Islands were straight ahead out there, then Iceland. I bet there was an open mic in Reykjavík.

Enough. I switched out the light.

Thank you and goodnight.